FIRST 50 SONGS

YOU SHOULD PLAY ON BANJO

Clawhammer arrangements by Michael J. Miles
Three-finger-style arrangements by Greg Cahill

ISBN 978-1-4950-5125-8

HAL•LEONARD®
CORPORATION
7777 W. BLUEMOUND RD. P.O. BOX 13819 MILWAUKEE, WI 53213

Visit Hal Leonard Online at
www.halleonard.com

TUNINGS

G MODAL TUNING (Clawhammer)

A-D-G-B-D TUNING (Clawhammer)

A-D-G-B-D TUNING (3-Finger-Style)

C TUNING (Clawhammer)

C MINOR TUNING (Clawhammer)

DOUBLE C TUNING (Clawhammer)

Angels from Montgomery

Words and Music by John Prine

G tuning:
(5th-1st) G-D-G-B-D

Key of G

Intro

Moderately slow

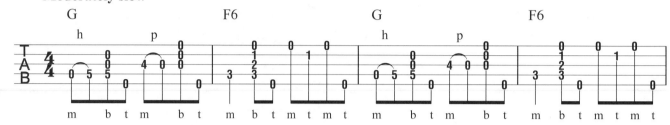

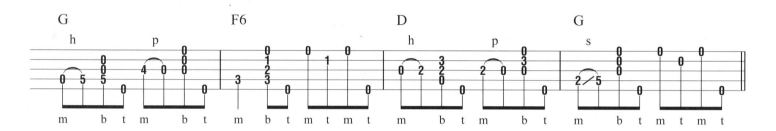

Verse

1. I am an old wom-an named af-ter my moth-er,
2., 3. *See additional lyrics*

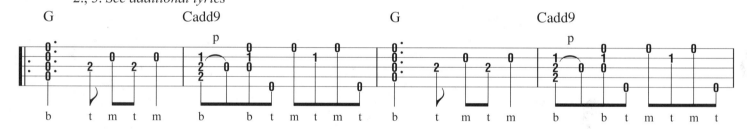

my old man's an - oth-er child that's grown old.

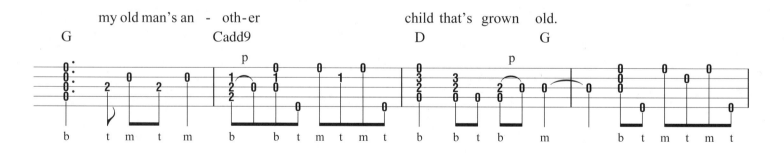

If dreams were thun-der and light-ning de - sire,

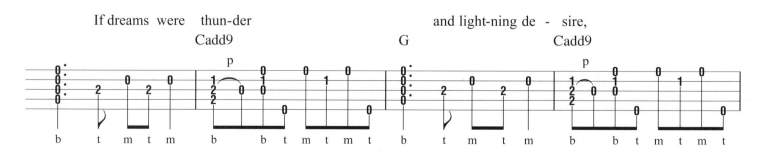

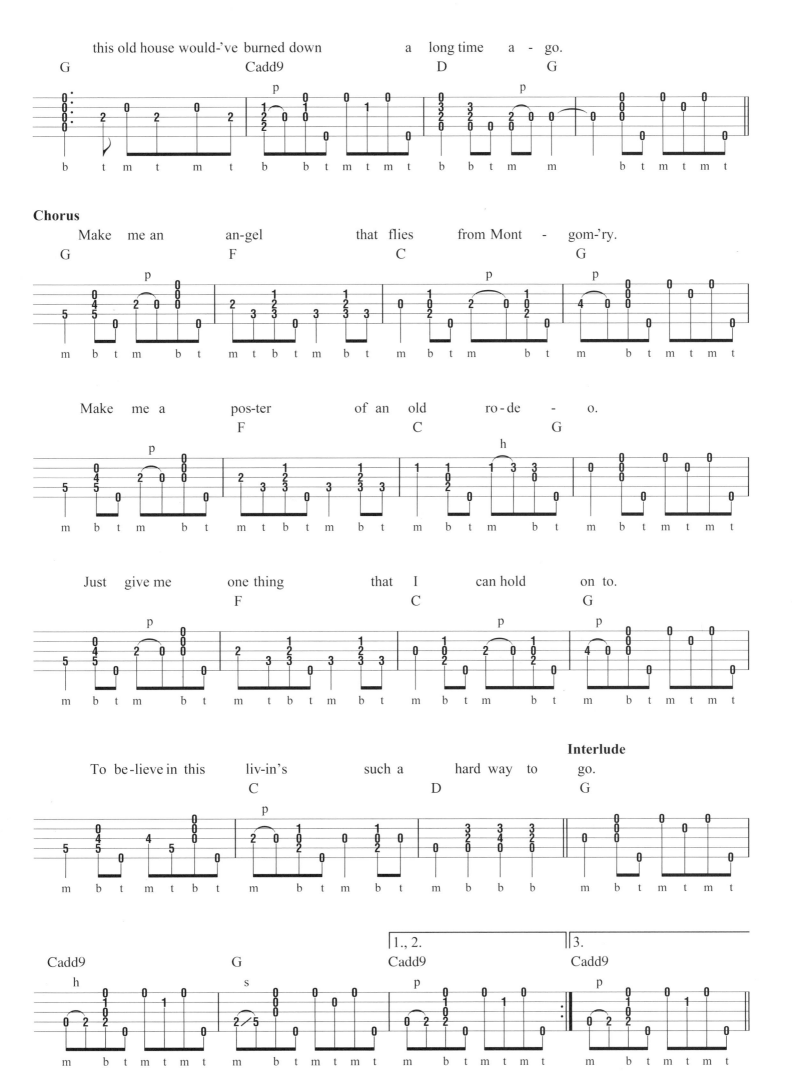

Chorus

Interlude

Banjo Break

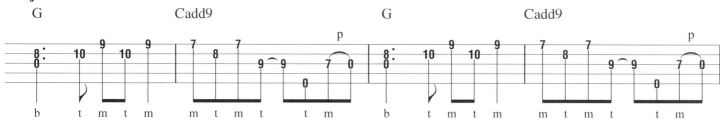

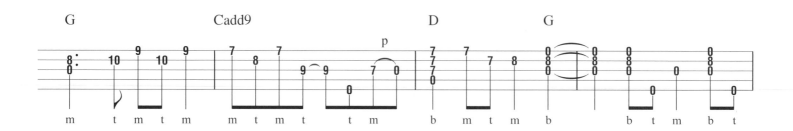

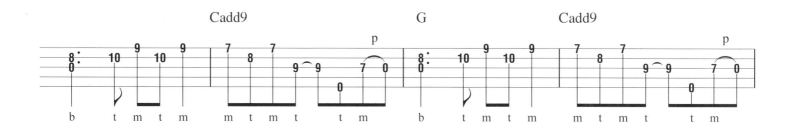

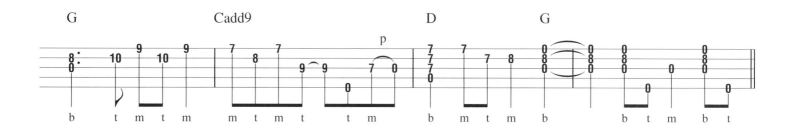

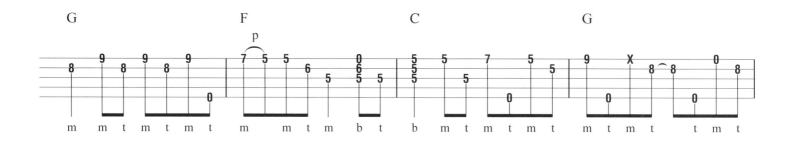

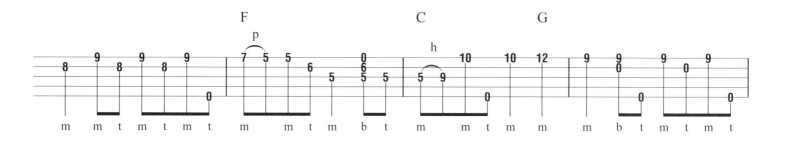

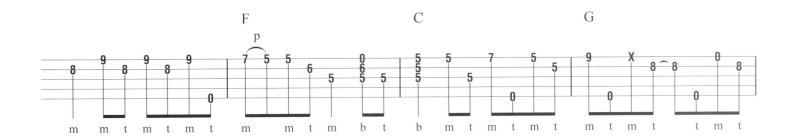

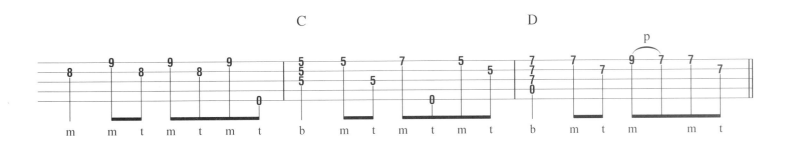

Outro

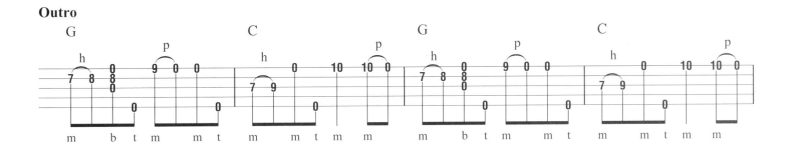

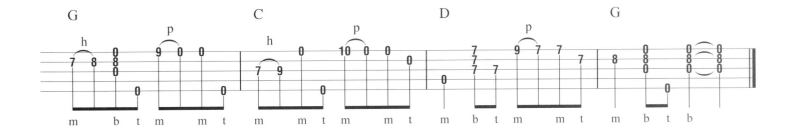

Additional Lyrics

2. When I was a young girl, well, I had me a cowboy.
   He weren't much to look at, just free rambling man.
   But that was a long time and no matter how I try,
   The years just flow by like a broken down dam.

3. There's flies in the kitchen, I can hear 'em there buzzing
   And I ain't done nothing since I woke up today.
   How the hell can a person go to work in the morning
   And come home in the evening and have nothing to say?

Big Yellow Taxi

Words and Music by Joni Mitchell

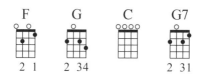

C tuning:
(5th-1st) G-C-G-C-E

Key of C

Intro

Moderately

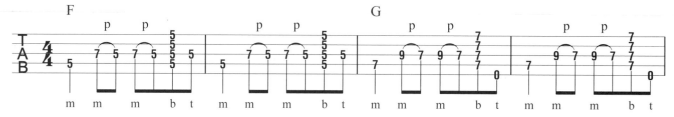

1. They

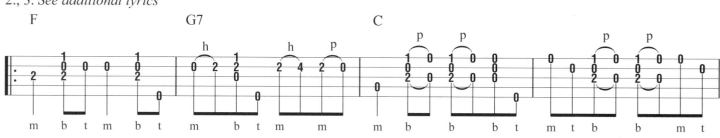

Verse

paved par - a - dise,   put up a   park - ing   lot   with a

2., 3. *See additional lyrics*

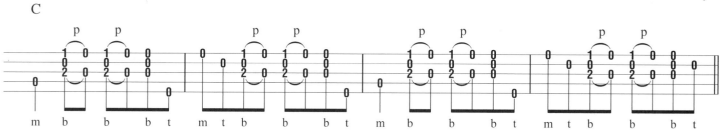

pink ho - tel, a   bou-tique and a swing-ing hot   spot.

Chorus

Don't it al-ways seem to go that you don't know what you got till it's gone? They

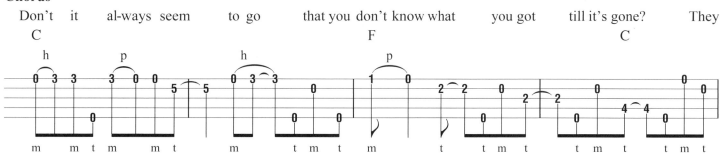

paved par - a - dise, put up a park - ing lot. They

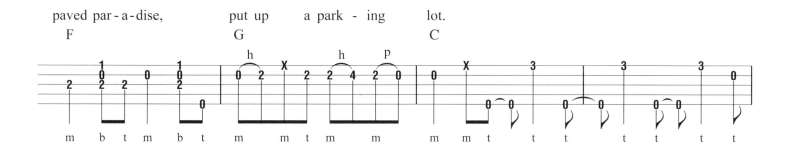

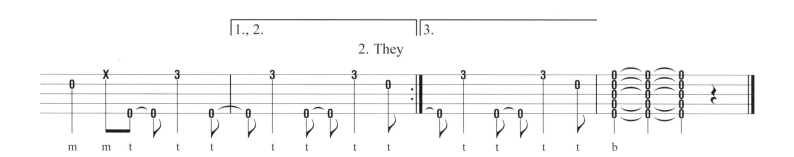

1., 2. | 3.

2. They

Additional Lyrics

2. They took all the trees
   And put 'em in a tree museum
   And they charged the people
   A dollar and a half to see 'em.

3. Hey farmer, farmer,
   Put away the DDT now.
   Give me spots on my apples
   But leave me the birds and the bees
   Please!

Blowin' in the Wind

Words and Music by Bob Dylan

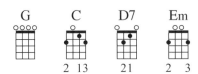

G   C   D7   Em

G tuning:
(5th-1st) G-D-G-B-D

Key of G

Moderately slow

𝄋 Verse

1. How man - y roads must a man walk down Be-
3. How man - y times must a man look up Be-

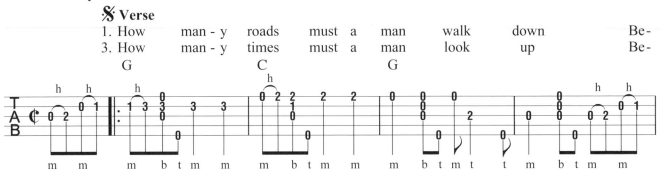

fore you call him a man? Yes, 'n'
fore he can see the sky? Yes, 'n'

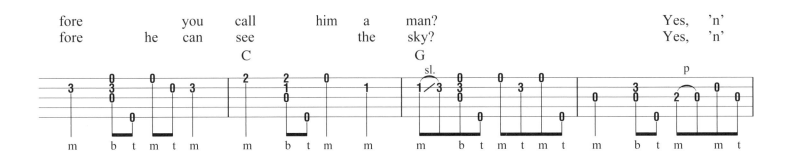

how man - y seas must a white dove sail Be -
how man - y ears must one man have Be -

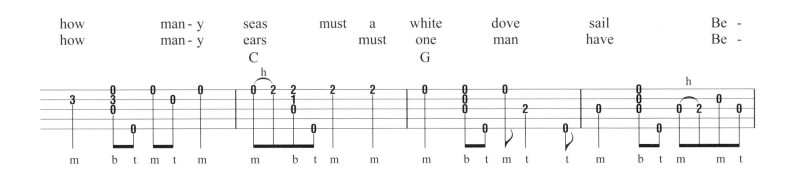

fore she sleeps in the sand? Yes, 'n'
fore he can hear peo - ple cry? Yes, 'n'

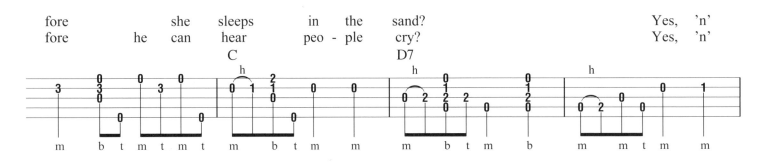

how man-y times must the can-non-balls fly Be -
how man-y deaths will it take till he knows That

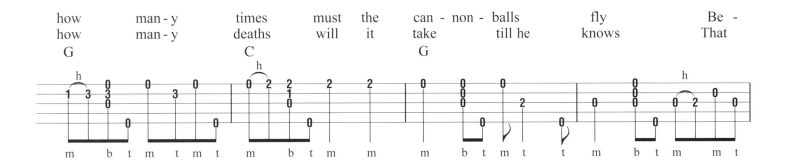

fore they're for - ev - er banned?
too man-y peo - ple have died? The

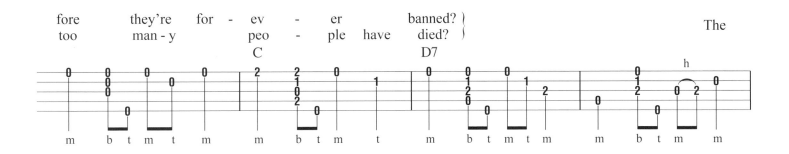

an - swer, my friend, is blow-in' in the wind The

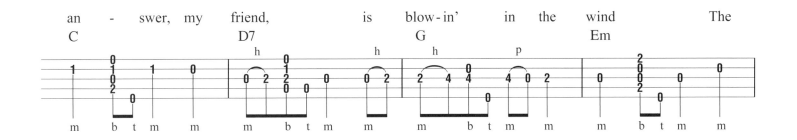

To Coda ⊕

an - swer is blow-in' in the wind

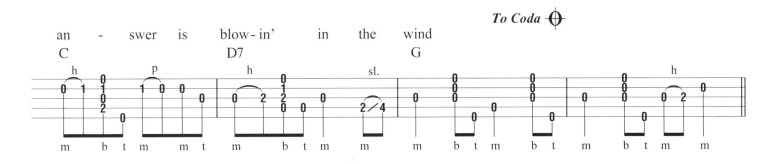

Interlude

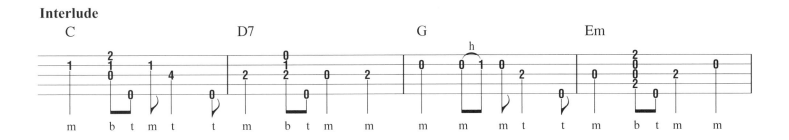

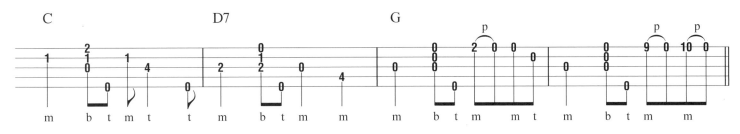

Verse

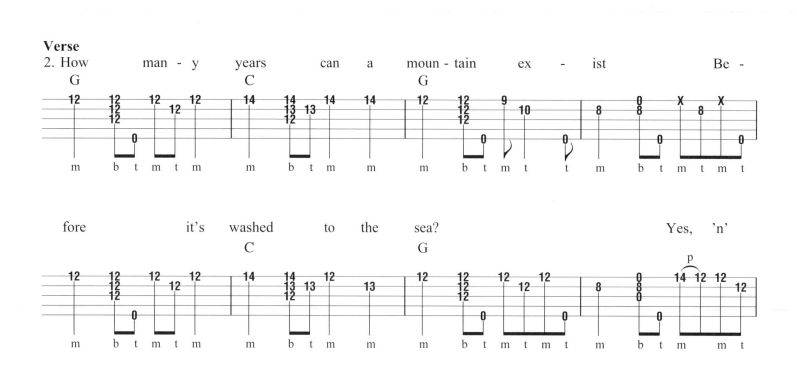

2. How man - y years can a moun - tain ex - ist Be -
fore it's washed to the sea? Yes, 'n'

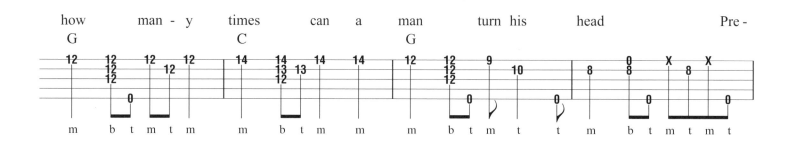

how man - y years can some peo - ple ex - ist Before they're al - lowed to be free? Yes, 'n'

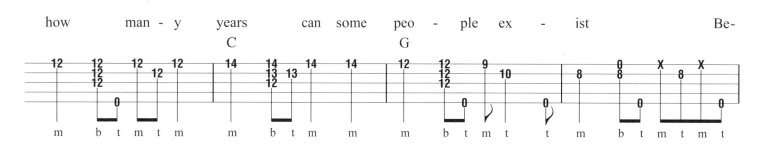

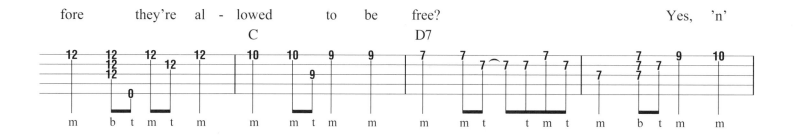

how man - y times can a man turn his head Pre-
tend - ing he just does - n't see? The

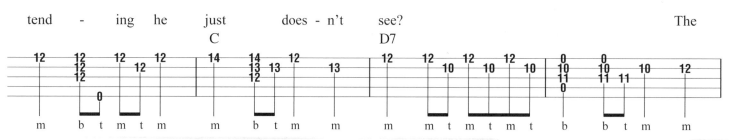

an - swer, my friend, is blow - in' in the wind The

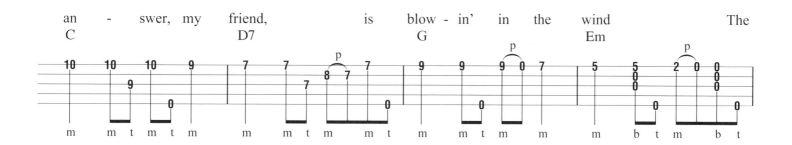

an - swer is blow - in' in the wind

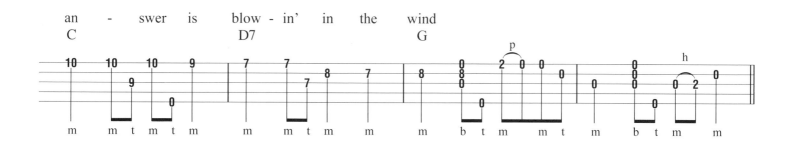

Interlude

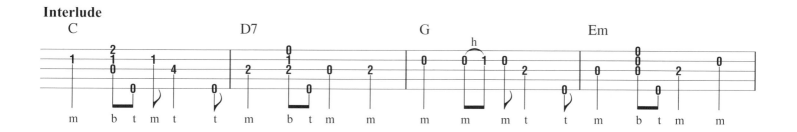

D.S. al Coda

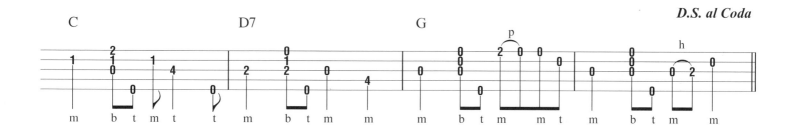

Coda

Outro

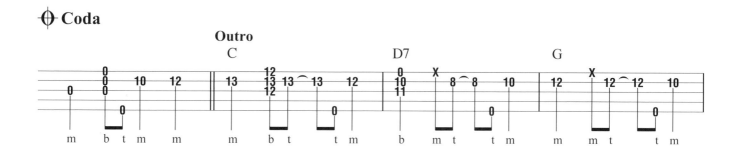

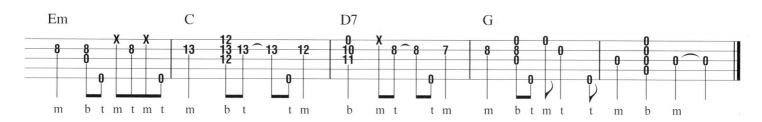

Candy Man Blues

Words and Music by "Mississippi" John Hurt

Double C tuning:
(5th-1st) G-C-G-C-D

Key of C

Moderately

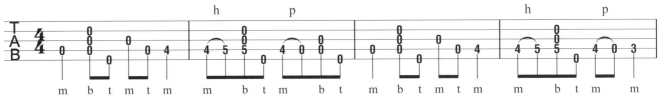

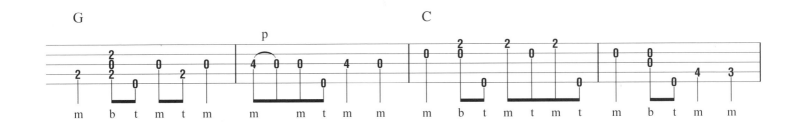

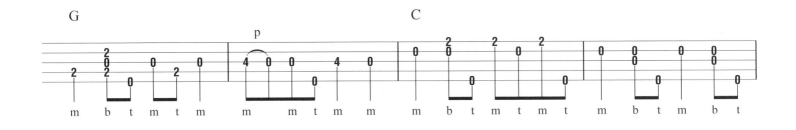

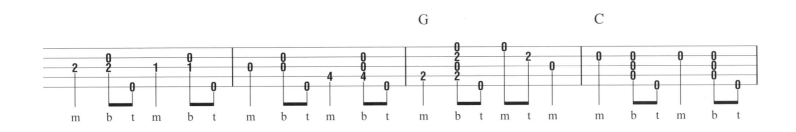

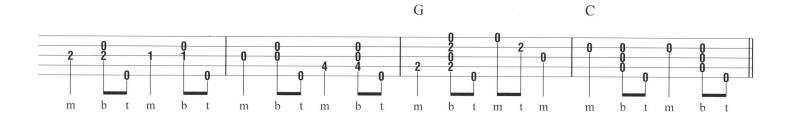

B Banjo Break

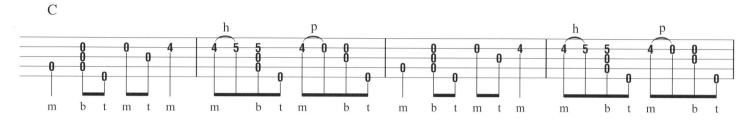

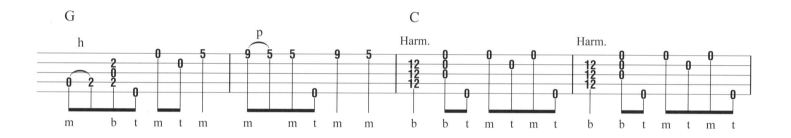

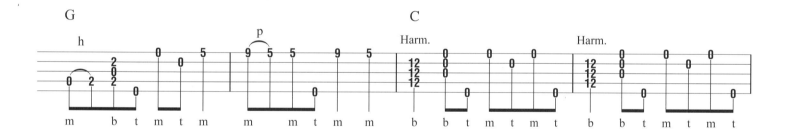

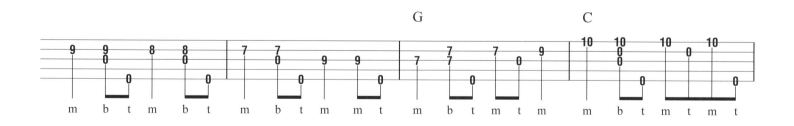

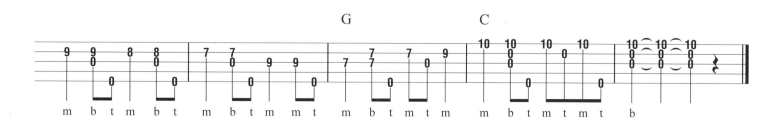

Carolina in My Mind

Words and Music by James Taylor

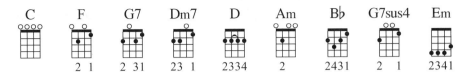

C tuning:
(5th-1st) G-C-G-C-E

Key of C
    Chorus
      Moderately

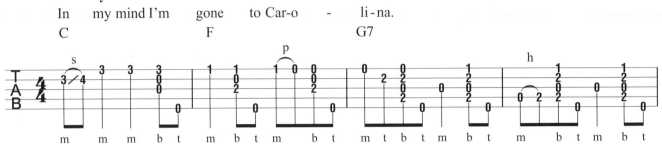

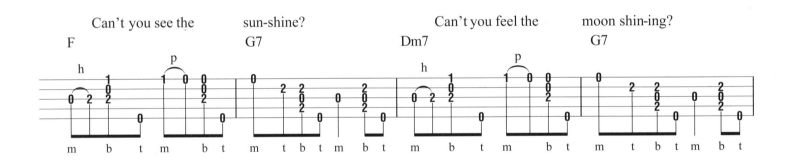

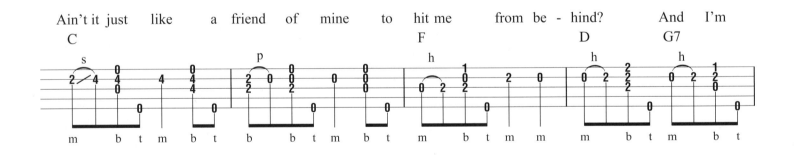

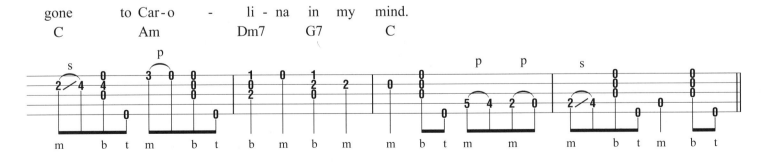

Verse

1. Kar-en, she's a sil - ver sun, you best walk a - way and watch it shin - ing.
2., 3. *See additional lyrics*

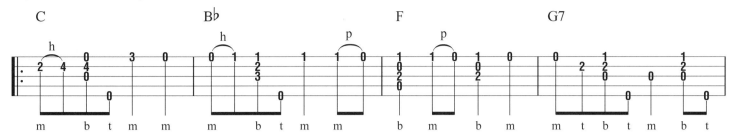

Watch her watch the morn-ing come a

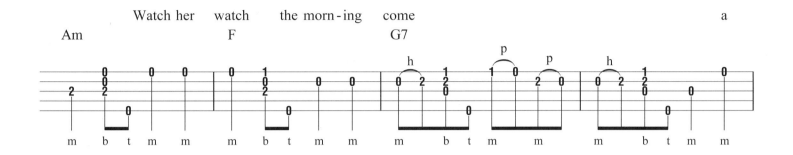

sil - ver tear ap - pear-ing. Now I'm cry - in', ain't I

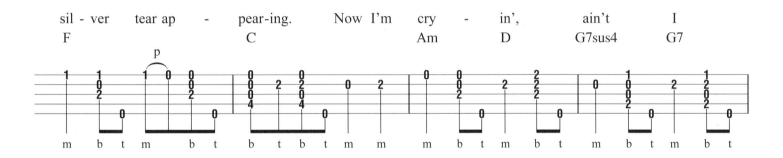

1.

To Coda ⊕

gone to Car-o - li - na in my mind. 2. There

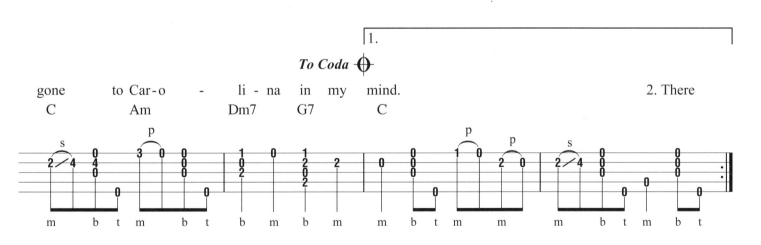

2.

D.C. al Coda ⊕ **Coda**

With a

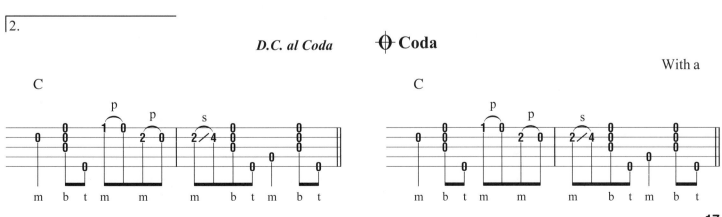

Bridge

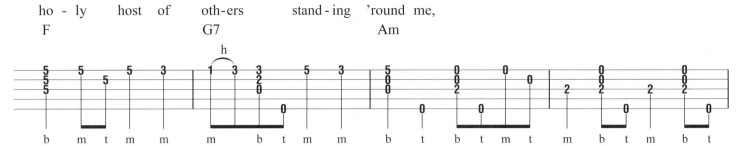

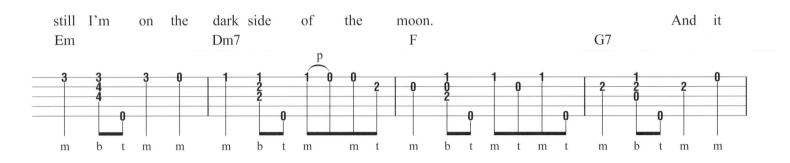

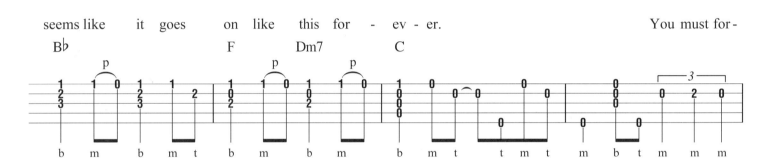

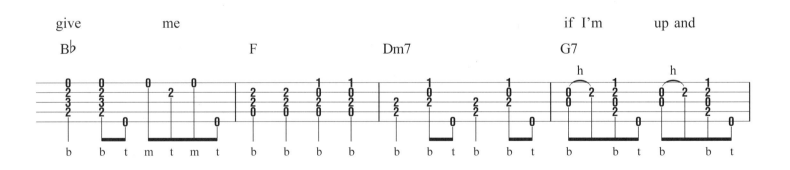

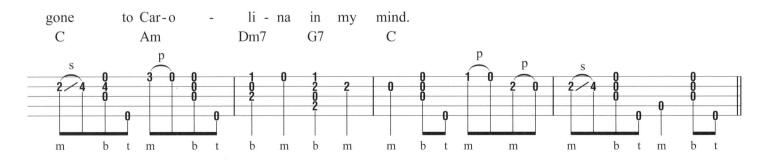

Chorus

In my mind I'm gone to Car-o - li-na. Can't you see the

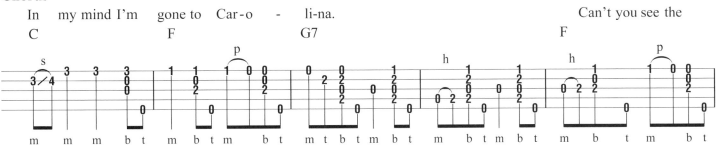

sun - shine? Can't you feel the moon shin-ing? Ain't it just like a

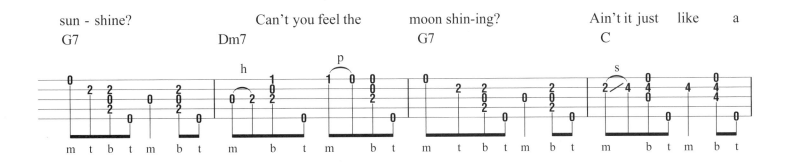

friend of mine to hit me from be - hind? And I'm gone to Car-o - li-na in my

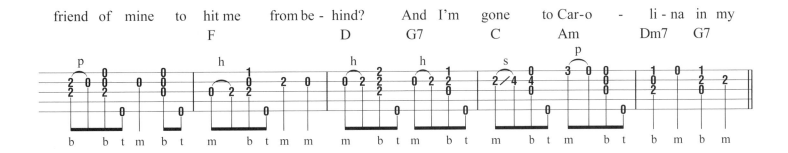

Repeat & fade

mind. Gone to Car - o - li - na in my

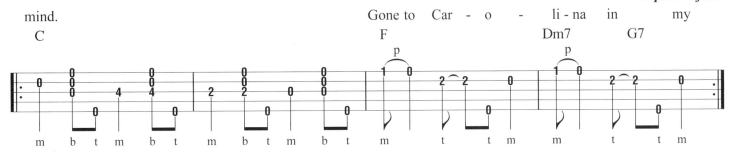

Additional Lyrics

2. There ain't no doubt in no one's mind
That love's the finest thing around.
Whisper something soft and kind
And hey, babe, the sky's on fire.
I'm dyin', ain't I?
I've gone to Carolina in my mind.

3. Dark and silent, late last night
I think I might have heard the highway call
And geese in flight and dogs that bite.
The signs that it might be omens
Say I'm going, going.
I've gone to Carolina in my mind.

Circles

Words and Music by Harry Chapin

C tuning:
(5th-1st) G-C-G-C-E

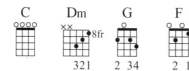

Key of C

Verse

Moderately

1., 4. All my life's a cir-cle, sun-rise and sun-down. The
2., 3. *See additional lyrics*

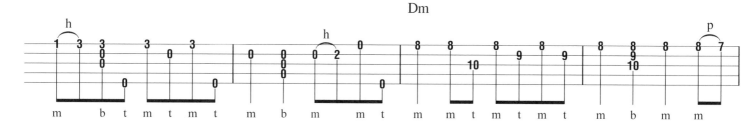

moon rolls through the night-time till the day-break comes a-round. All my life's a

cir-cle but I can't tell you why. The sea-sons spin-nin'

'round a-gain; the years keep roll-in' by.

Additional Lyrics

2. It seems like I've been here before;
I can't remember when.
But I got this funny feeling
That I'll be back once again.
There's no straight lines make up my life
And all my roads have bends.
There's no clear-cut beginnings
And so far no dead-ends.

3. I've found you a thousand times,
I guess you've done the same.
But then we lose each other;
It's just like a childrens' game;
But as I see you here again,
A thought runs through my mind;
Our love is like a circle,
Let's go 'round one more time.

Key to the Highway

Words and Music by Big Bill Broonzy and Chas. Segar

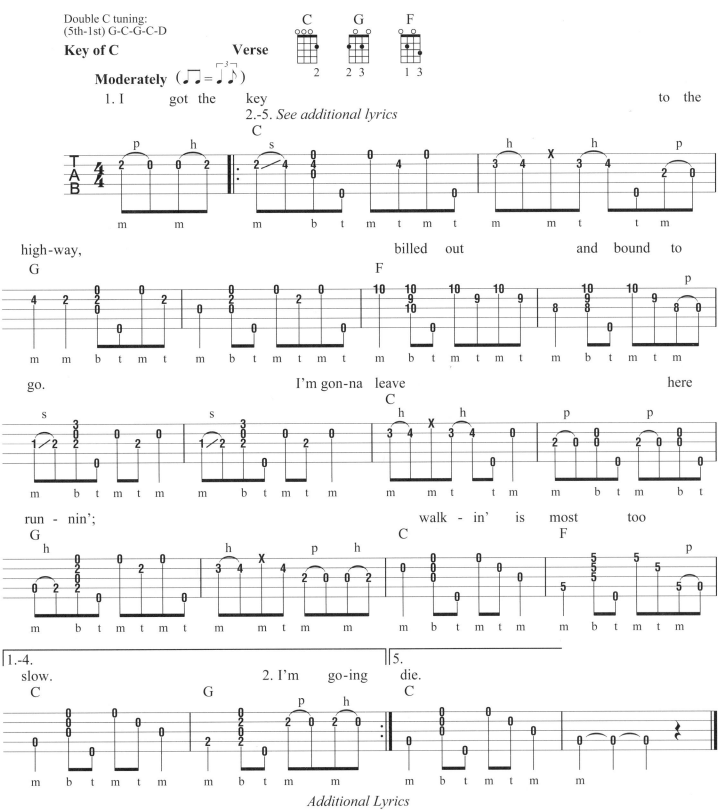

Additional Lyrics

2. I'm going back, to the border
   Where I'm better known
   Because you haven't done nothing baby,
   Except drove a good man away from home.

3. When the moon peeks over the mountains,
   Baby, I'm gonna be on my way.
   I'm gonna roam the mean old highway
   Until the break of day.

4. So give me one,
   Give one more kiss baby,
   'Cause when I leave this town
   I won't be back no more, no more.

5. So goodbye, goodbye baby
   Baby, I must, I must, I must say goodbye
   'Cause I'm a roam this mean old highway
   Until the day I die.

City of New Orleans

Words and Music by Steve Goodman

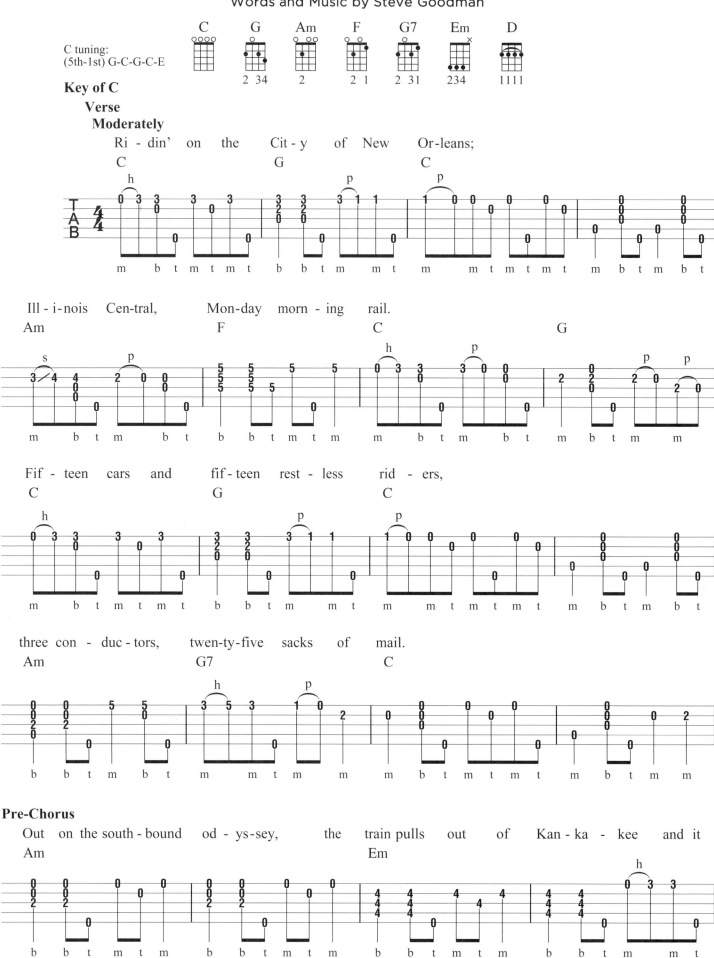

C tuning:
(5th-1st) G-C-G-C-E

Key of C

Verse

Moderately

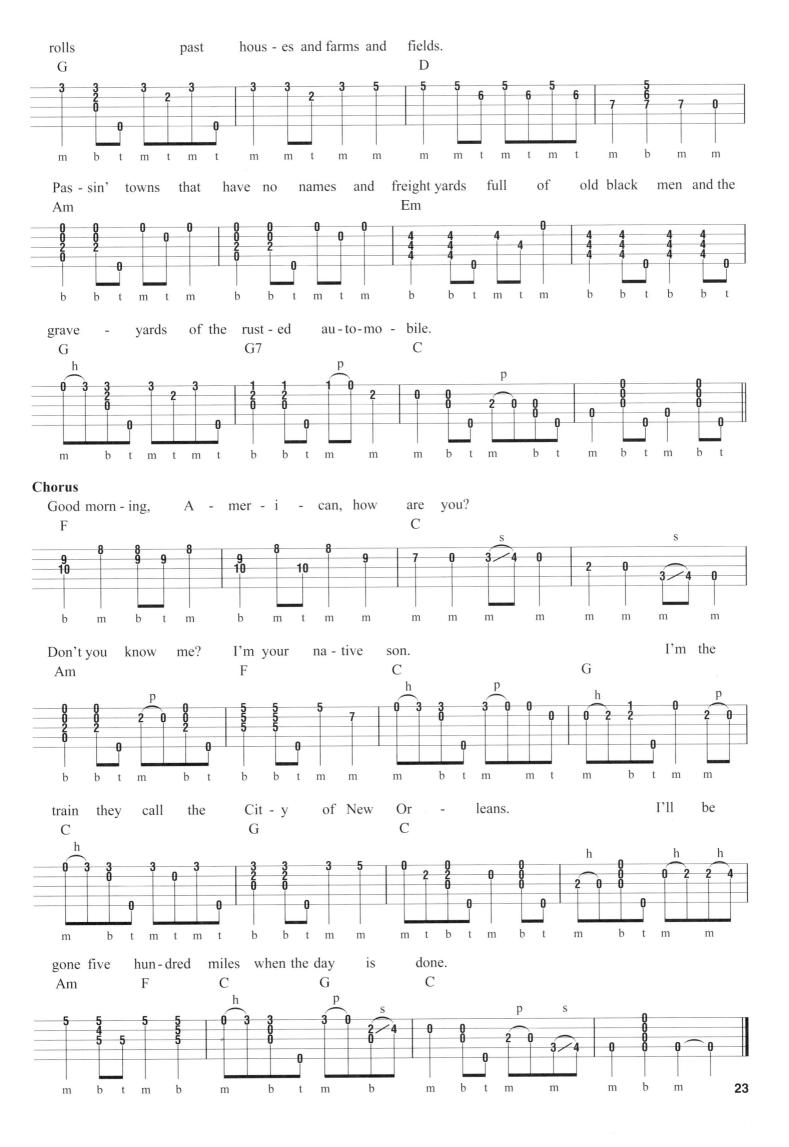

Cluck Old Hen

Traditional

G5

G modal tuning:
(5th-1st) G-D-G-C-D

Key of Gm

Moderately fast

G5

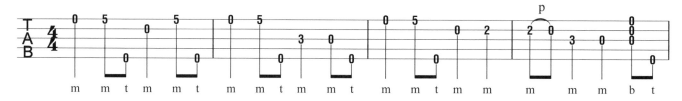

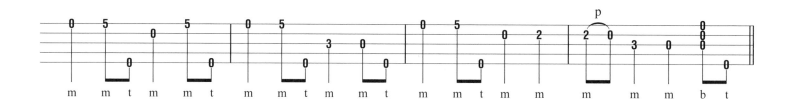

 G5

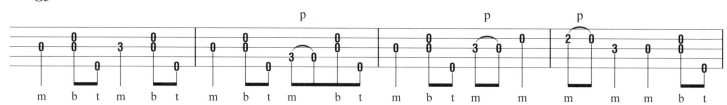

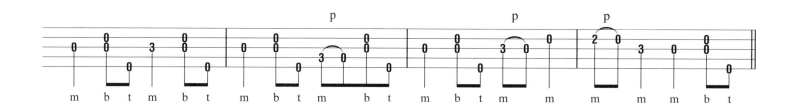

C | Banjo Break

G5

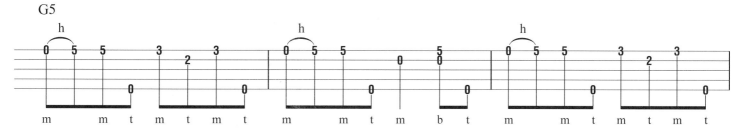

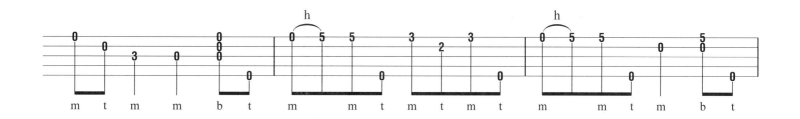

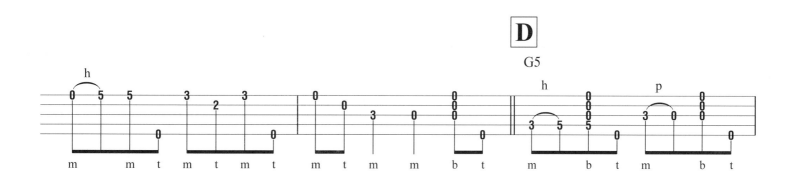

D

G5

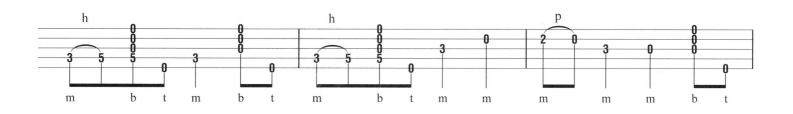

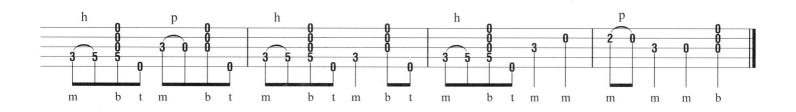

Freight Train

Words and Music by Elizabeth Cotten

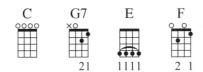

C tuning:
(5th–1st) G-C-G-C-E

Key of C

Verse
Fast

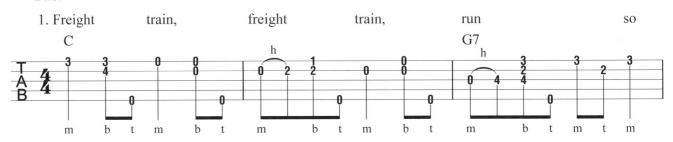

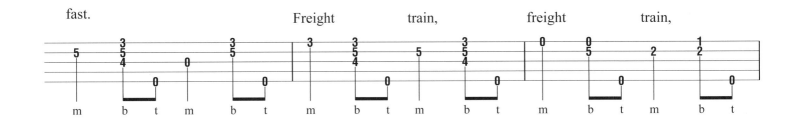

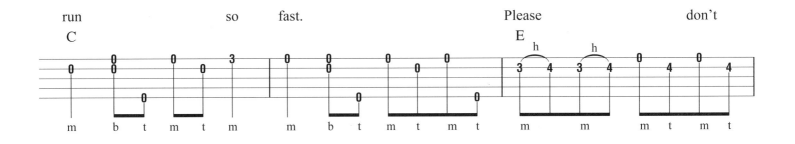

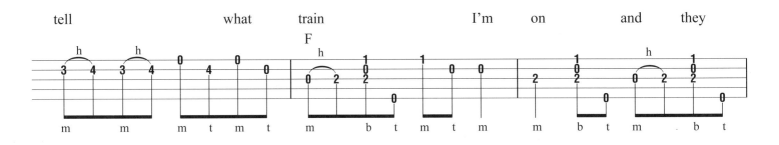

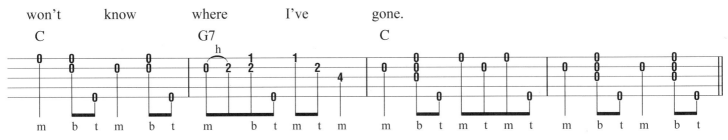

Banjo Break

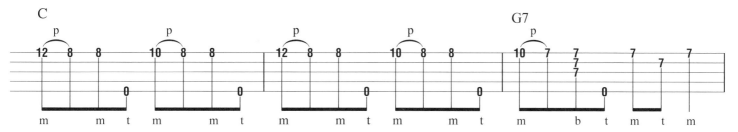

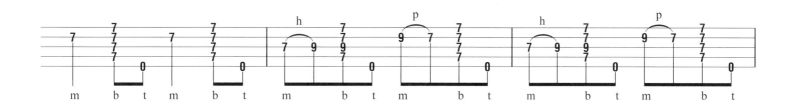

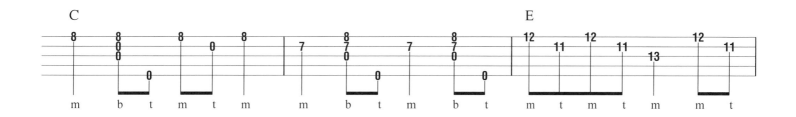

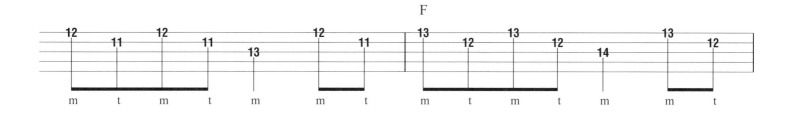

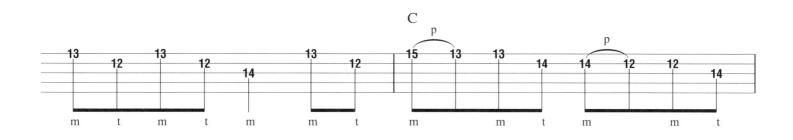

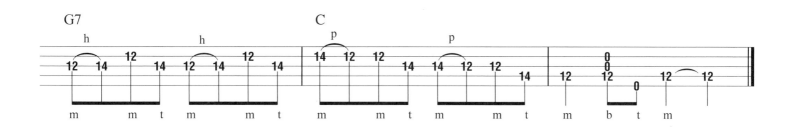

Going Down the Road
(I Ain't Going to Be Treated This Way)

Words and Music by Woody Guthrie and Lee Hays

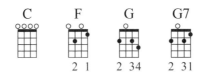

C tuning:
(5th-1st) G-C-G-C-E

Key of C
  Verse
   Moderately fast

Goin' down   the   road   feel-in'   bad,

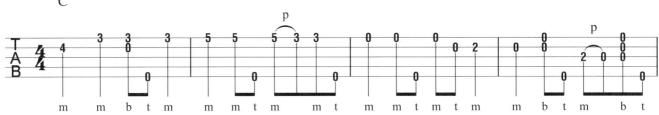

goin' down   that   road   feel - in'   bad.

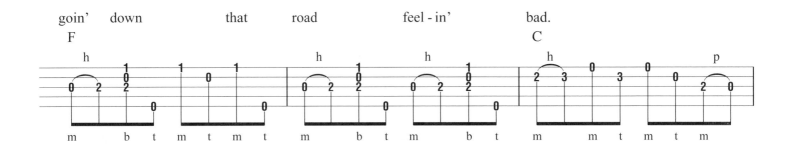

Goin'   down   that   road   feel - in'

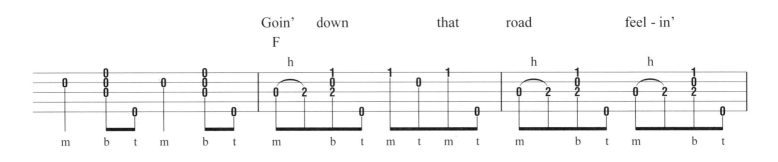

bad,   Lord,   Lord.   Oh   I   ain't   gon - na   be

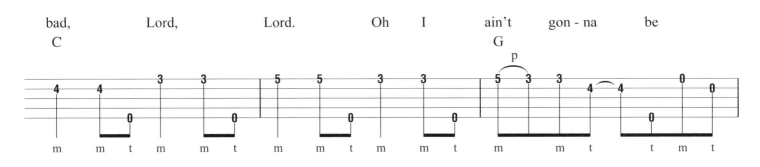

treat-ed   this   a -   way.

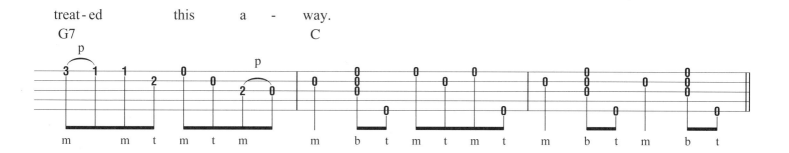

Banjo Break

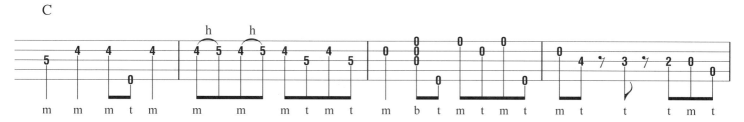

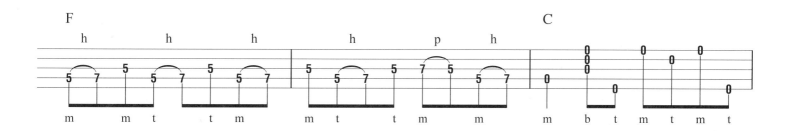

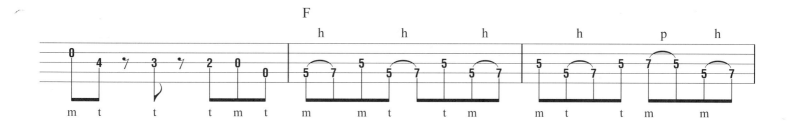

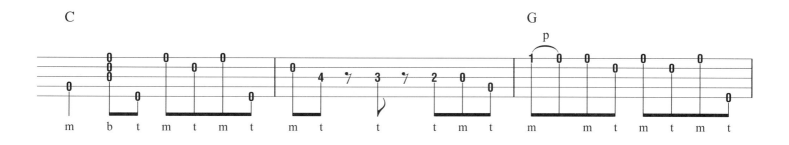

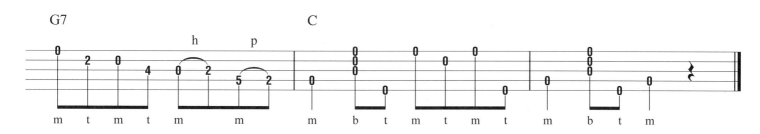

The House of the Rising Sun

Words and Music by Alan Price

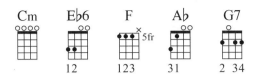

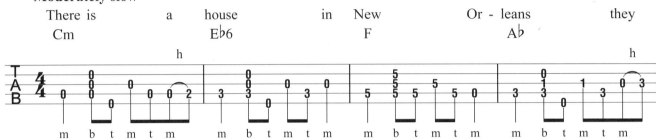

Cm tuning:
(5th-1st) G-C-G-C-Eb

Key of Cm
Verse
Moderately slow

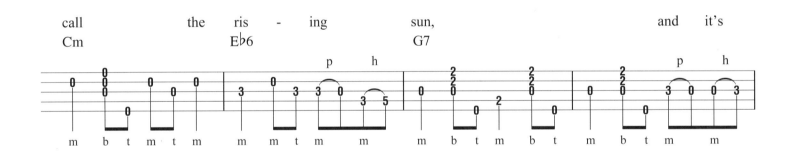

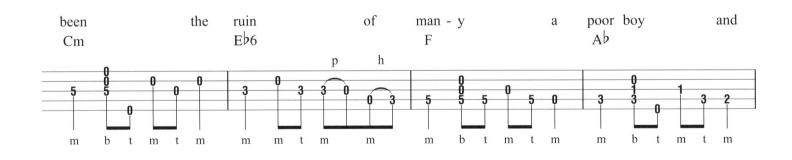

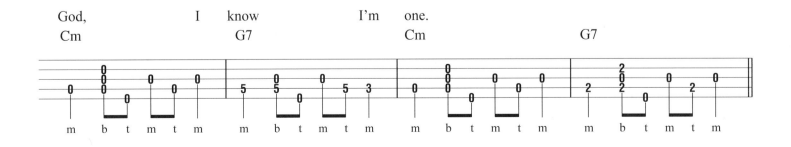

Banjo Break

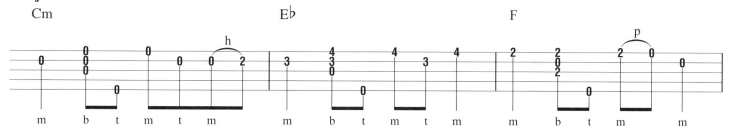

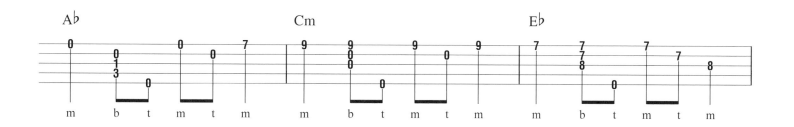

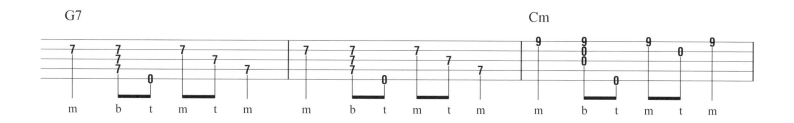

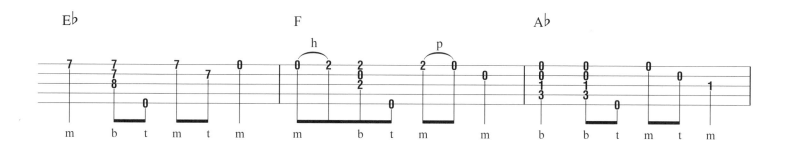

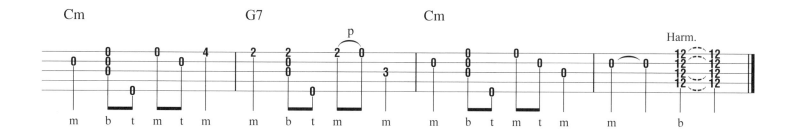

I Know You Rider

Traditional
Arranged by Jerry Garcia, Keith Godchaux, William Kreutzmann,
Phil Lesh, Ronald McKernan and Bob Weir

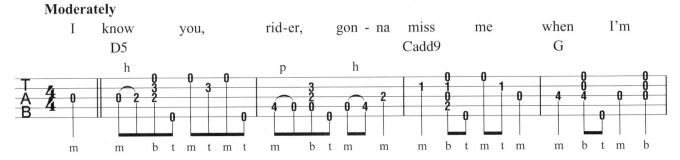

Tuning:
(5th-1st) A-D-G-B-D

Key of D

Chorus/Verse

Moderately

I know you, rid-er, gon-na miss me when I'm

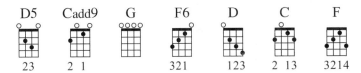

gone. I

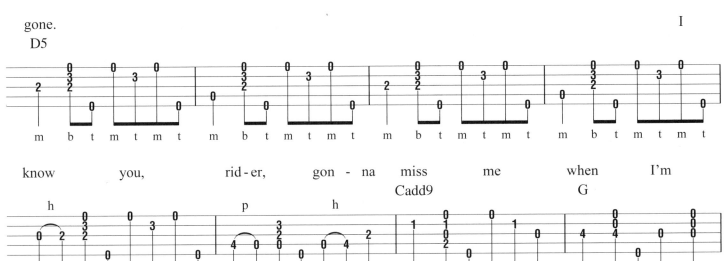

know you, rid-er, gon-na miss me when I'm

gone. Gon-na

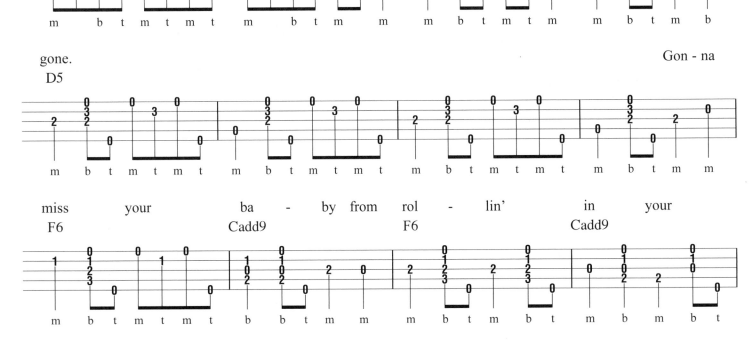

miss your ba - by from rol - lin' in your

arms.

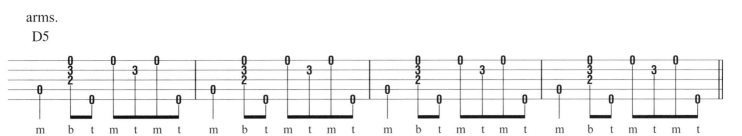

Banjo Break

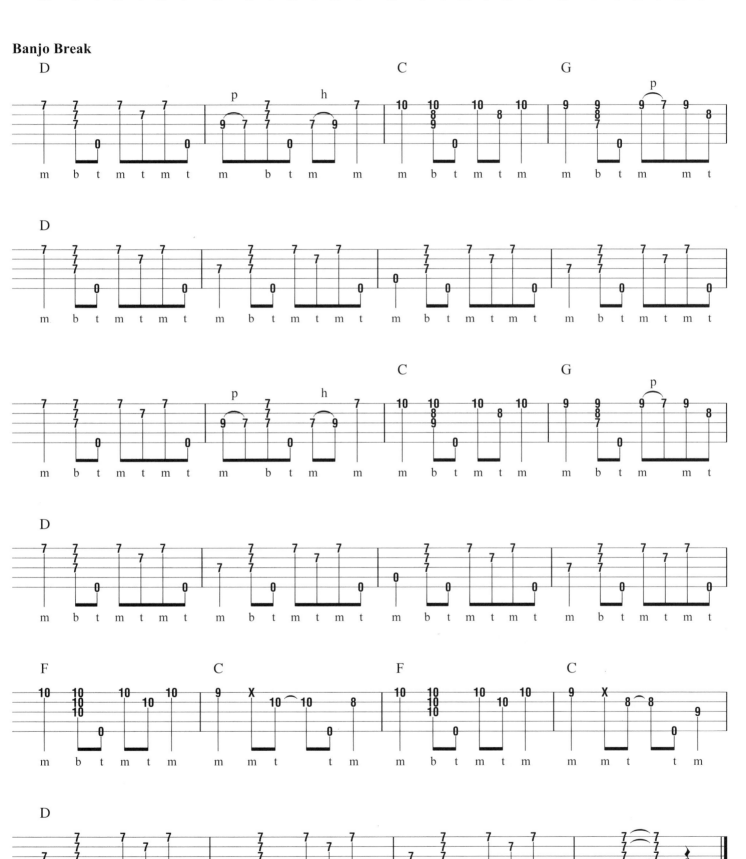

If I Had a Hammer
(The Hammer Song)

Words and Music by Lee Hays and Pete Seeger

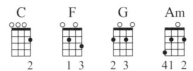

Double C tuning:
(5th-1st) G-C-G-C-D

Key of C

Verse

Moderately

1. If   I   had a   ham - mer,   I'd   ham-mer in the
2., 3., 4. *See additional lyrics*

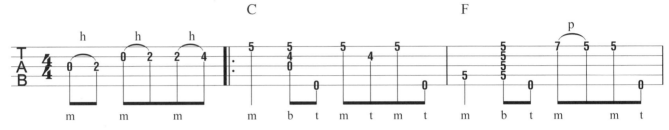

morn - ing.   I'd   ham-mer in the   eve - ning

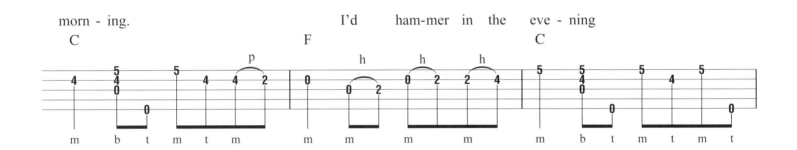

all   o - ver this   land.   I'd   ham-mer out

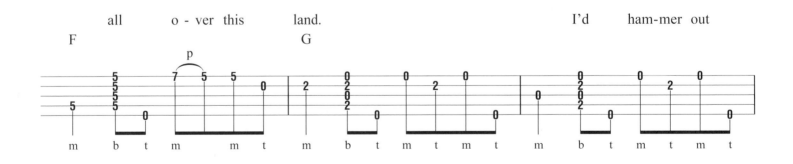

dan - ger,   I'd   ham-mer out   warn - ing.

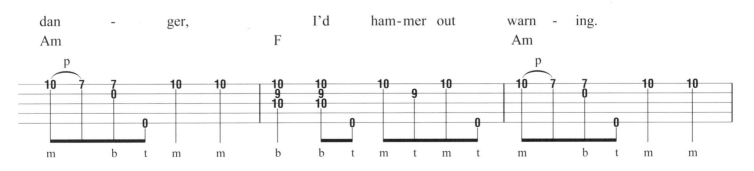

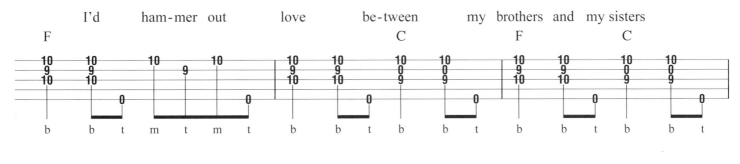

I'd   ham-mer out   love   be-tween   my brothers and my sisters

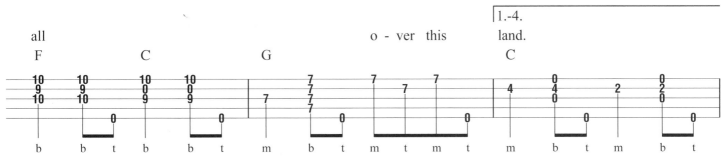

all   o - ver this   land.

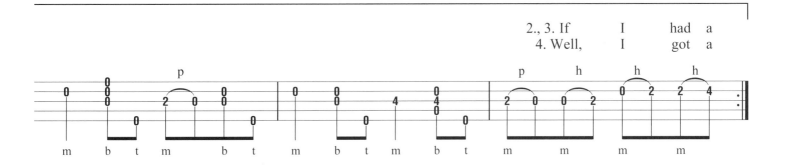

1.-4.

2., 3. If   I   had a
4. Well,   I   got a

5.
land.

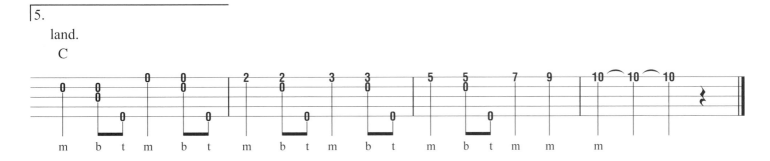

Additional Lyrics

2. If I had a bell, I'd ring it in the morning.
   I'd ring it in the evening, all over this land.
   I'd ring out danger, I'd ring out a warning.
   I'd ring out love between my brothers and my sisters
   All over this land.

3. If I had a song, I'd sing it in the morning
   I'd sing it in the evening, all over this land.
   I'd sing out danger, I'd sing out warning.
   I'd sing out love between my brothers and my sisters
   All over this land.

4. Well I got a hammer, and I got a bell,
   And I got a song to sing, all over this land.
   It's the hammer of justice, it's the bell of freedom.
   It's the song about love between my brothers and my sisters,
   All over this land.

The Last Thing on My Mind

Words and Music by Tom Paxton

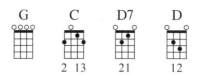

G tuning:
(5th-1st) G-D-G-B-D

Key of G

Verse

Moderately

1. It's a les-son too late for the learn-ing
2., 3. *See additional lyrics*

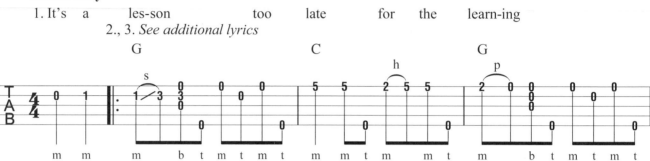

made of sand, made of sand. In the

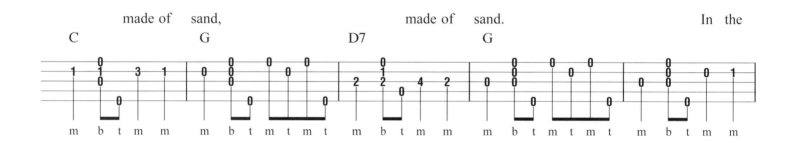

wink of an eye, my soul is turn-ing in your

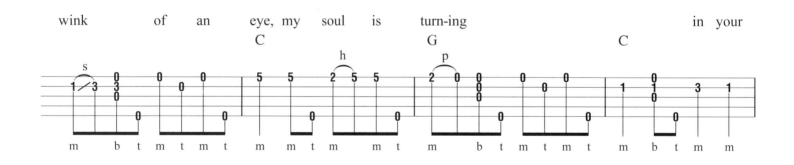

hand, in your hand. Are you

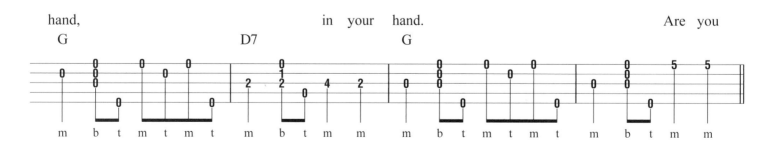

Chorus

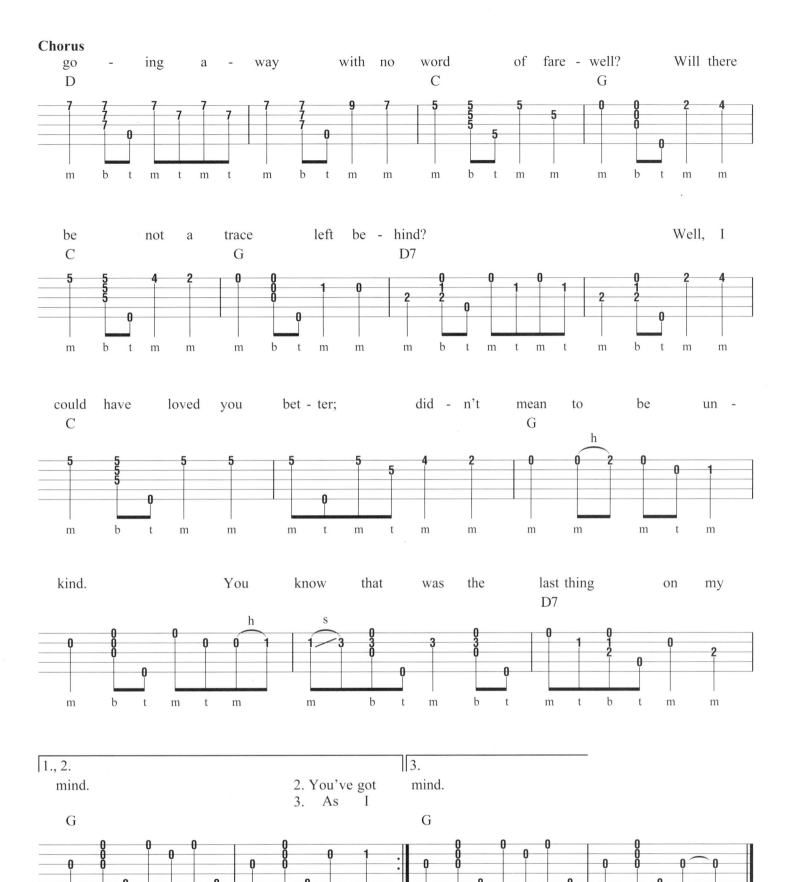

Additional Lyrics

2. You've got reasons a-plenty for going,
   This I know, this I know.
   For the weeds have been steadily growing.
   Please don't go, please don't go.

3. As I lie in my bed in the morning
   Without you, without you,
   Each song in my breast dies a-borning
   Without you, without you.

Maple Leaf Rag

Music by Scott Joplin

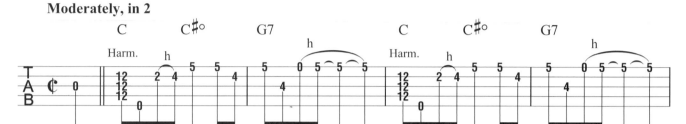

Double C tuning:
(5th-1st) G-C-G-C-D

Key of C

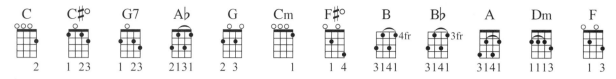

Moderately, in 2

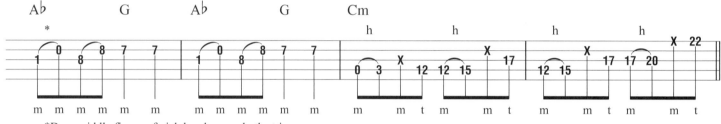

*Drag middle finger of pick hand across both strings.

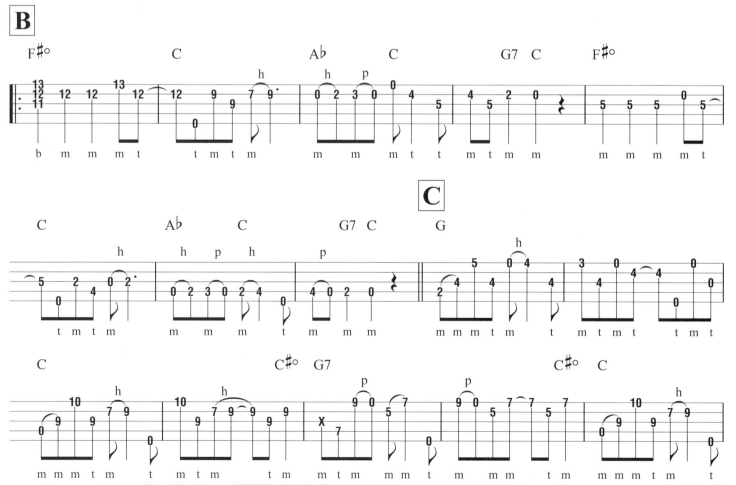

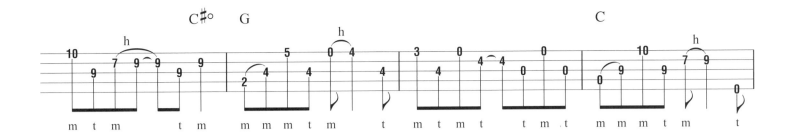

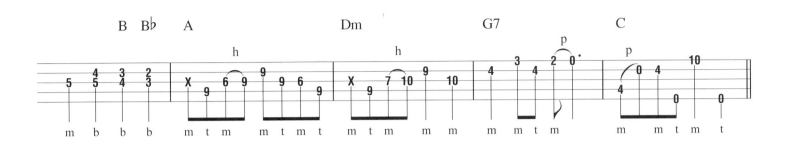

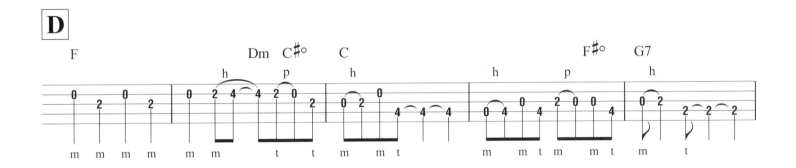

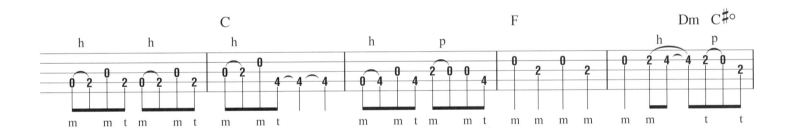

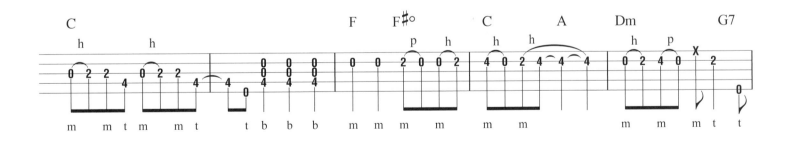

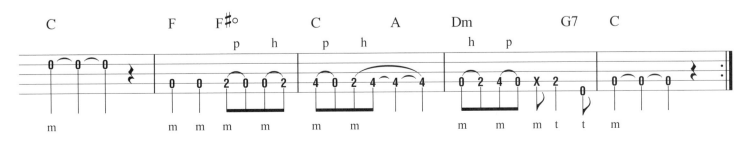

Minuet in G

from THE ANNA MAGDALENA NOTEBOOK (originally for keyboard)
By Johann Sebastian Bach

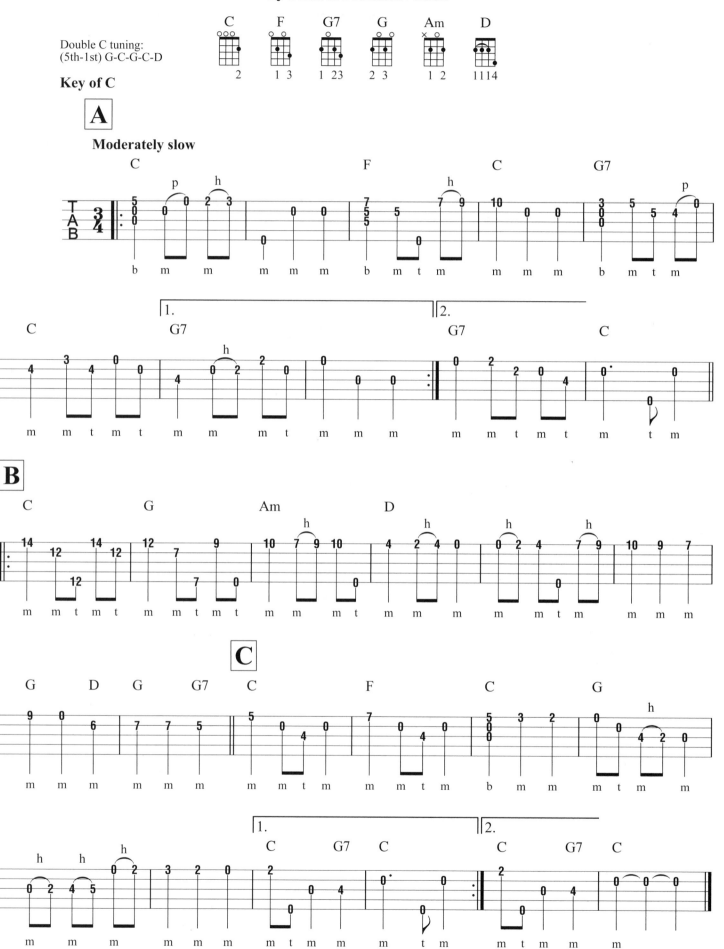

Mr. Bojangles

Words and Music by Jerry Jeff Walker

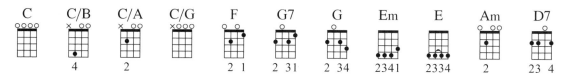

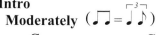

C tuning:
(5th-1st) G-C-G-C-E

Key of C

Intro
Moderately

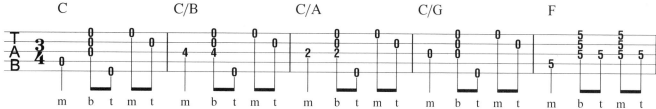

Verse

1. I knew a man, Bo - jan-gles, and he
2., 3., 4. *See additional lyrics*

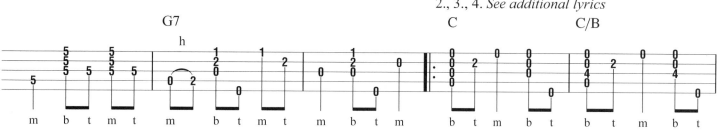

danced for you in worn out shoes.

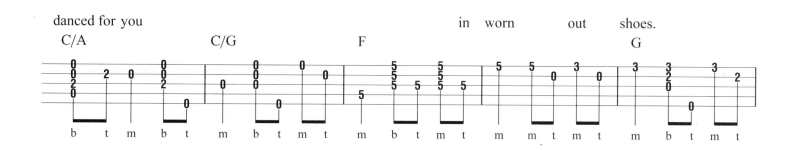

Sil-ver hair, a rag-ged shirt and bag-gy pants,

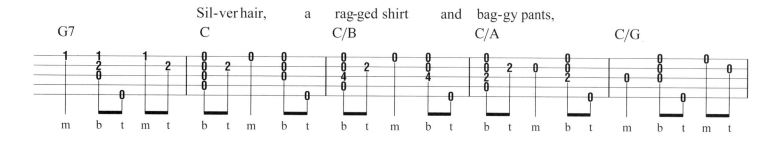

41

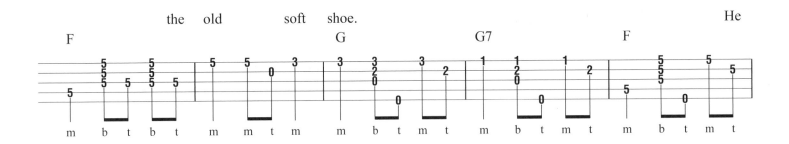

the old   soft shoe.   He

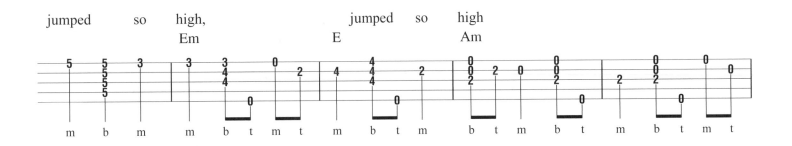

jumped   so   high,   jumped   so   high

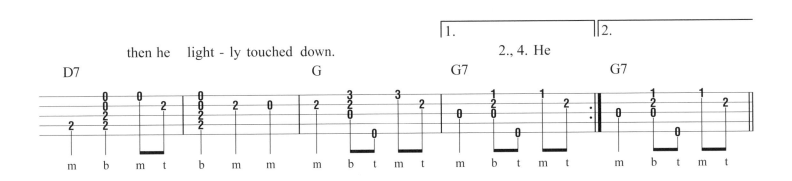

then he   light - ly touched down.   2., 4. He

Chorus

Mis-ter Bo   -   jan - gles,

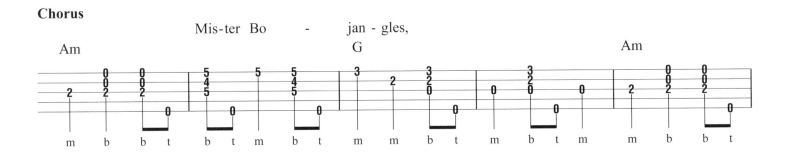

Mis-ter Bo   -   jan - gles,   Mis-ter Bo -

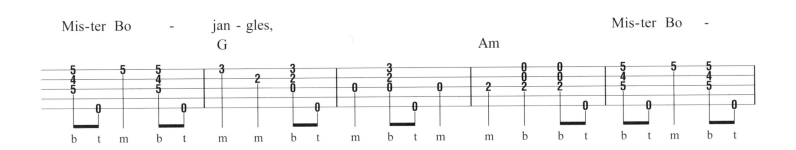

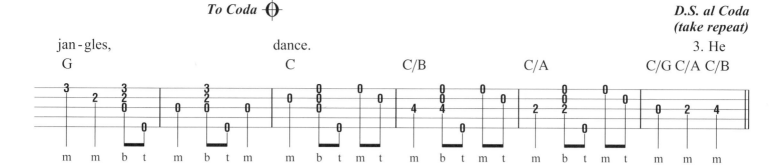

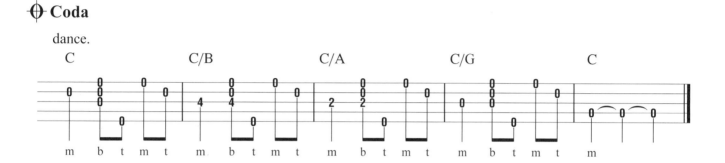

⊕ **Coda**

Additional Lyrics

2. He said his name, "Bojangles," and he danced a lick, across the cell.
   He grabbed his pants and spread his stance, oh he jumped so high then he clicked his heels.
   He let go a laugh, let go a laugh;
   Shook back his clothes all around.

3. He danced for those at minstrel shows and county fairs throughout the south.
   He spoke with tears of fifteen years how his dog and he traveled about.
   The dog up and died, he up and died;
   After twenty years he still grieves.

4. He said, "I dance now at every chance in honky tonks for drinks and tips,
   But most the time I spend behind these county bars, 'cause I drinks a bit."
   He shook his head, and as he shook his head,
   I heard someone ask him, please...

Mr. Tambourine Man

Words and Music by Bob Dylan

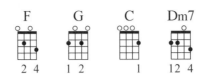

Double C tuning:
(5th–1st) G-C-G-C-D

Key of C

Chorus
Moderately

Hey! Mis- ter Tam - bou - rine Man, play a song for me I'm not

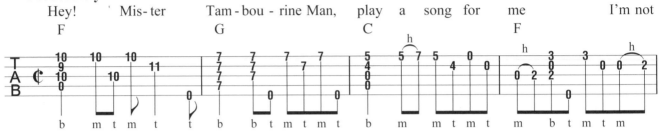

sleep - y and there is no place I'm go - ing to

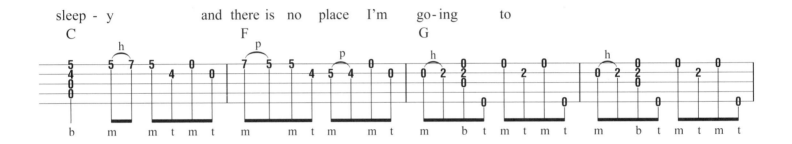

Hey! Mis- ter Tam - bou - rine Man, play a song for me In the

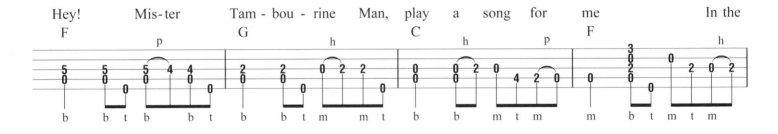

jing - le jang - le morn - ing I'll come fol - low-in' you 1. Though I

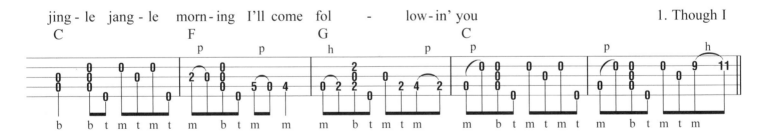

Verse

know that eve - nin's em - pire has re - turned in - to sand
2., 3. 4. *See additional lyrics*

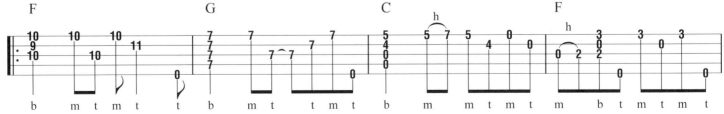

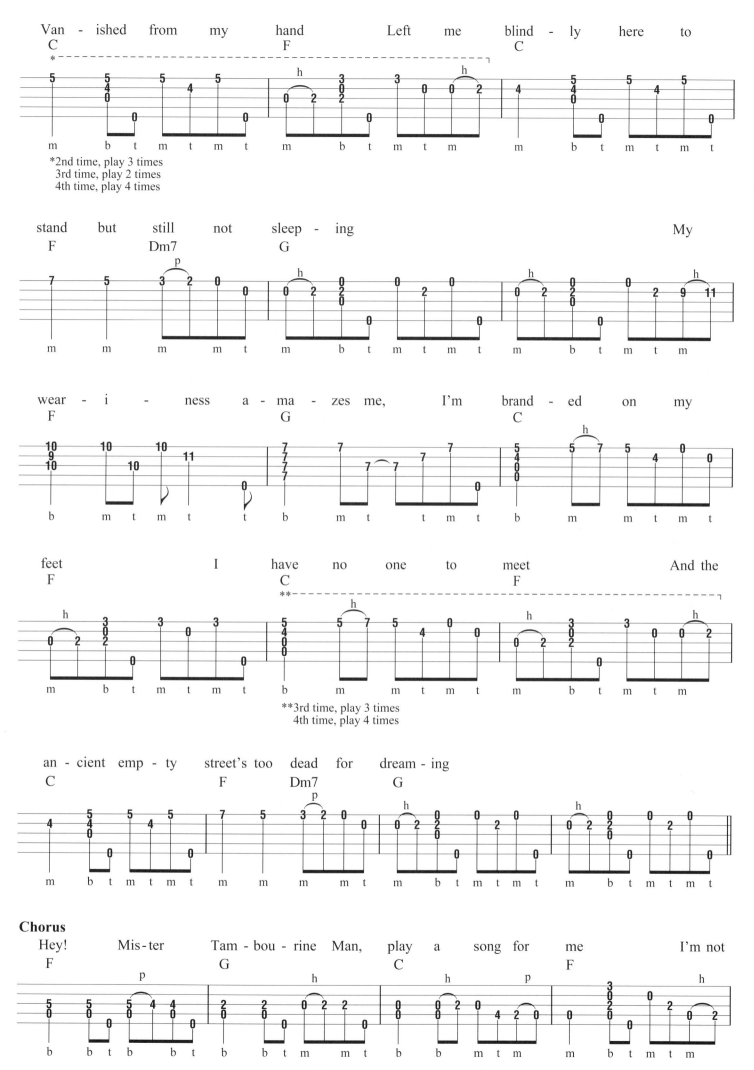

sleep-y   and there   is   no   place   I'm   go-ing   to

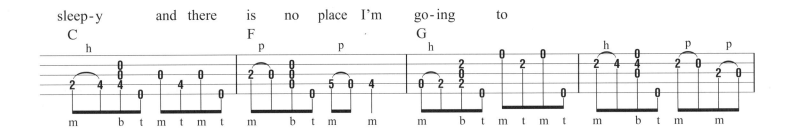

Hey!   Mis-ter   Tam - bou - rine Man,   play   a   song   for   me   In the

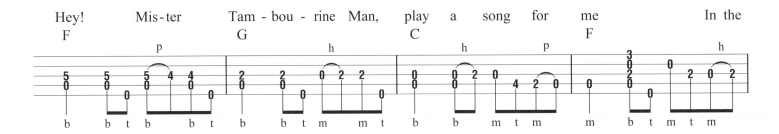

jin - gle   jan - gle   morn - ing   I'll come   fol   -   low-in' you

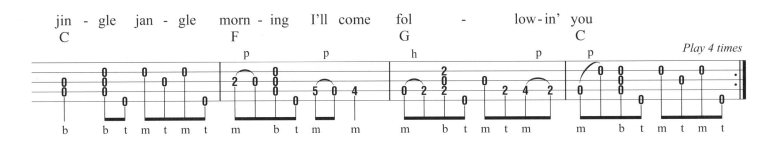

Outro

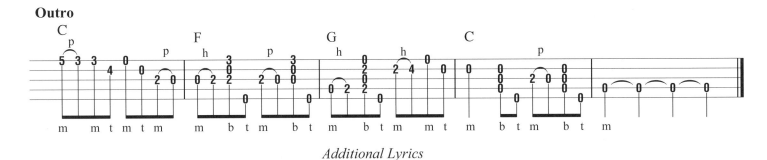

Additional Lyrics

2. Take me on a trip upon your magic swirlin' ship
My senses have been stripped, my hands can't feel to grip
My toes too numb to step
Wait only for my boot heels to be wanderin'
I'm ready to go anywhere, I'm ready for to fade
Into my own parade, cast your dancing spell my way
I promise to go under it

3. Though you might hear laughin', spinnin', swingin' madly across the sun
It's not aimed at anyone, it's just escapin' on the run
And but for the sky there are no fences facin'
And if you hear vague traces of skippin' reels of rhyme
To your tambourine in time, it's just a ragged clown behind
I wouldn't pay it any mind
It's just a shadow you're seein' that he's chasing

4. Then take me disappearin' through the smoke rings of my mind
Down the foggy ruins of time, far past the frozen leaves
The haunted, frightened trees, out to the windy beach
Far from the twisted reach of crazy sorrow
Yes, to dance beneath the diamond sky with one hand waving free
Silhouetted by the sea, circled by the circus sands
With all memory and fate driven deep beneath the waves
Let me forget about today until tomorrow

The M.T.A.

Words and Music by Jacqueline Steiner and Bess Hawes

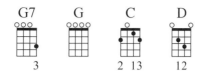

G tuning:
(5th-1st) G-D-G-B-D

Key of G
    Intro
       Moderately fast

1. Let me

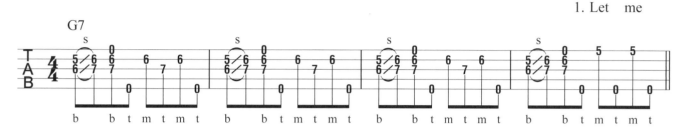

Verse

tell you of the stor-y of a man named Char-lie on a

2.-5. *See additional lyrics*

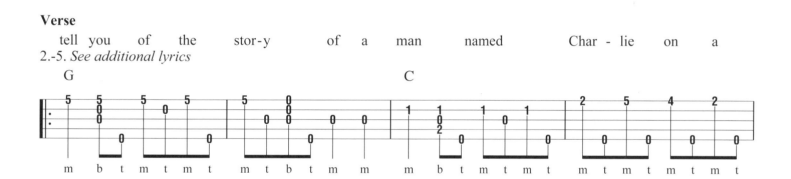

trag-ic and fate-ful day.   He put

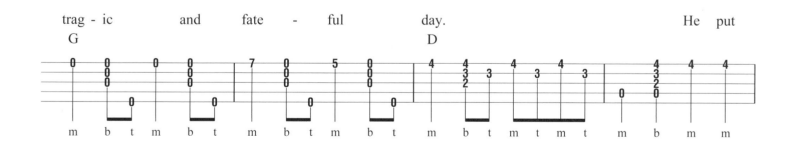

ten cents in his pock-et, kissed his wife and fam-'ly, went to

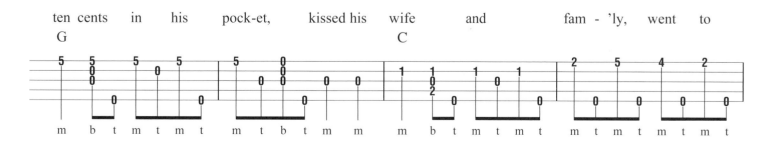

ride on the M. T. A.

2.-4. But did he
5. or else he'll

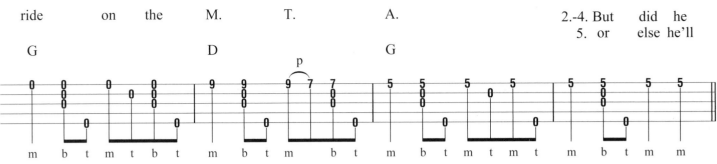

Chorus

ev - er re - turn? No, he nev - er re - turned,
nev - er re - turn, no he'll nev - er re - turn, and his

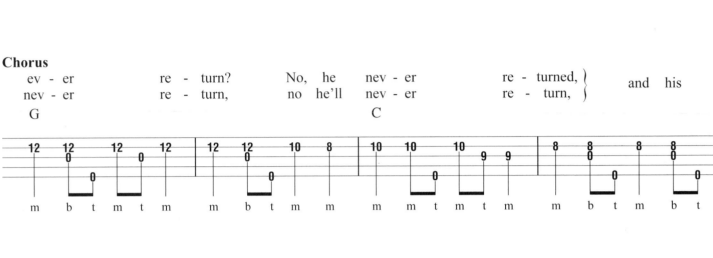

fate is still un - learned. (Poor old Char-lie.) He may

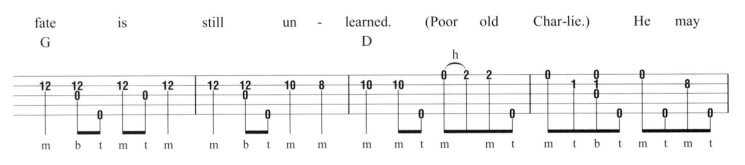

ride for - ev - er 'neath the streets of Bos-ton. He's the

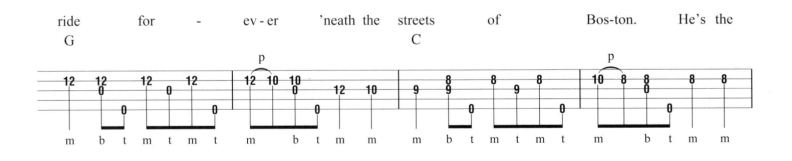

1.-4.

man who nev - er re - turned. 2. Char - lie

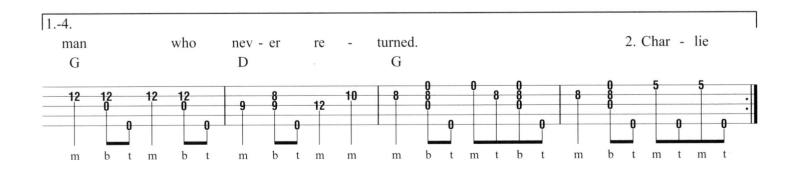

48

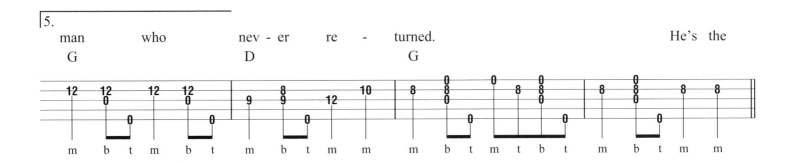

man   who   nev - er   re -   turned.   He's the

Repeat & fade

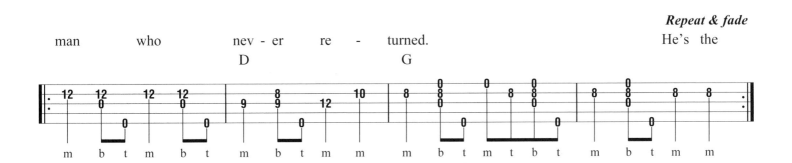

man   who   nev - er   re -   turned.   He's the

Additional Lyrics

2. Charlie handed in his dime at the Kendall Square station
   And he changed for Jamaica Plain.
   When he got there, the conductor told him, "One more nickel."
   Charlie couldn't get off of that train.

3. Now, all night long, Charlie rides through the station
   Crying, "What will become of me?
   How can I afford to see my sister in Chelsea
   Or my cousin in Roxbury?"

4. Charlie's wife goes down to the Sculley Square station
   Every day at quarter past two
   And through the open window, she hands Charlie a sandwich
   As the train comes rumbling through.

5. Now, you citizens of Boston,
   Don't you think it's a scandal,
   How the people have to pay and pay?
   Fight the fare increase, vote for George O'Brian.
   Get poor Charlie off the M.T.A.

Norwegian Wood
(This Bird Has Flown)

Words and Music by John Lennon and Paul McCartney

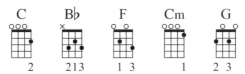

Double C tuning:
(5th-1st) G-C-G-C-D

Key of C

Verse

Moderately

1. I once had a girl, or should I
2., 3. *See additional lyrics*

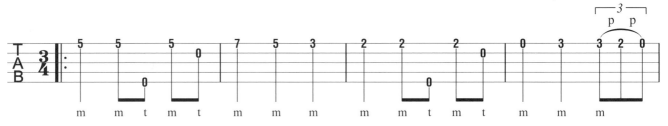

say, she once had me.

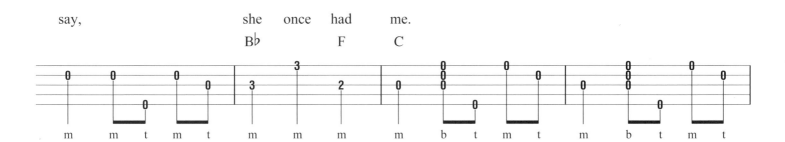

She showed me her room. Is - n't it

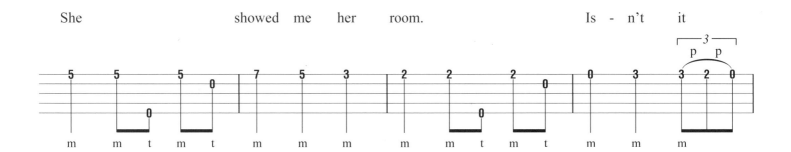

To Coda ⊕

good, Nor - we - gian wood? 1. She

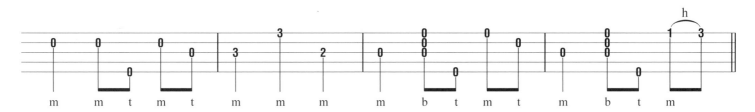

Bridge

asked me to stay and she told me to sit a - ny -

See additional lyrics

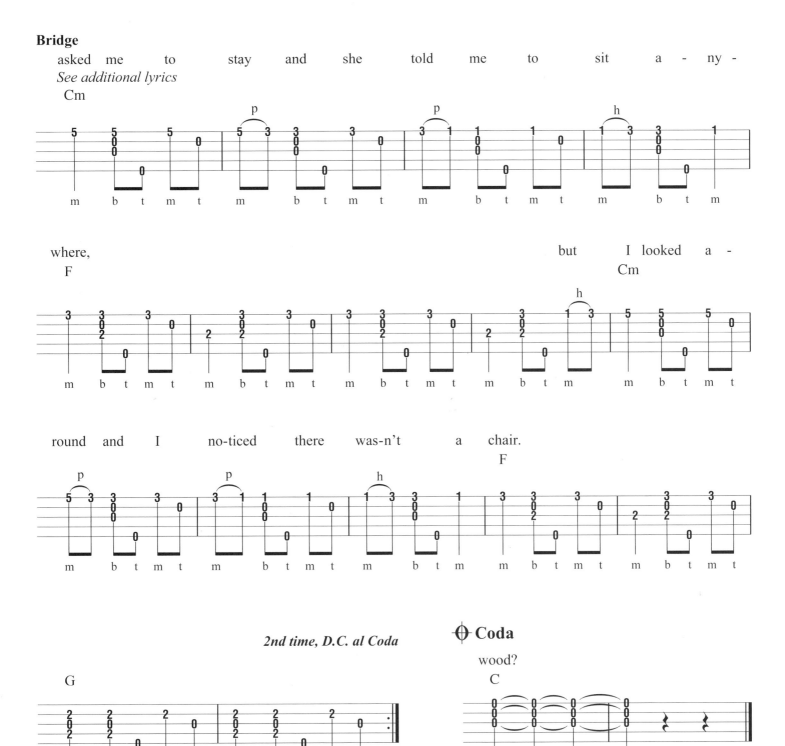

where,

but I looked a -

round and I no-ticed there was-n't a chair.

2nd time, D.C. al Coda

Coda

wood?

Additional Lyrics

2. I sat on her rug, biding my time, drinking her wine.
   We talked until two, and then she said, "It's time for bed."

Bridge: She told me she worked in the morning and started to laugh.
   I told her, I didn't, and crawled off to sleep in the bath.

3. And when I awoke, I was alone. This bird had flown.
   So, I lit a fire. Isn't it good, Norwegian Wood?

Shady Grove

Appalachian Folk Song

G modal tuning:
(5th-1st) G-D-G-C-D

Key of Gm

Chorus

Moderately, in 2

Shad - y Grove, my lit - tle love, Shad - y Grove I

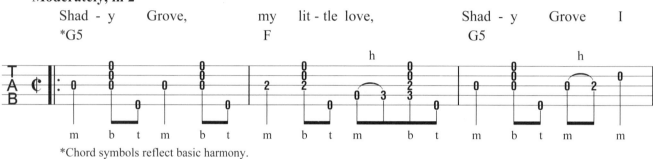

*Chord symbols reflect basic harmony.

say, Shad - y Grove, my lit - tle love, I'm

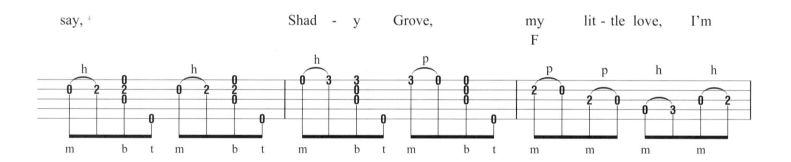

To Coda ⊕

bound to go a - way.

Verse

1. Cheeks as red as a
2.-5. *See additional lyrics*

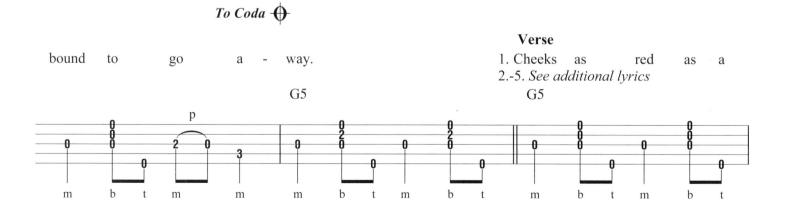

bloom - in'   rose,   eyes   are   the pret - ti - est   brown.

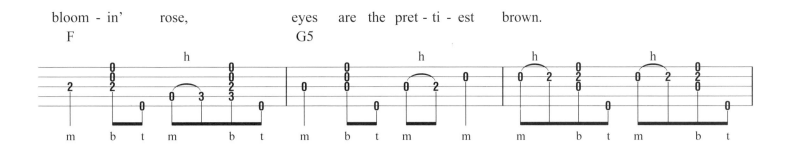

She's   the   dar - ling   of   my   heart,   sweet - est   girl   in

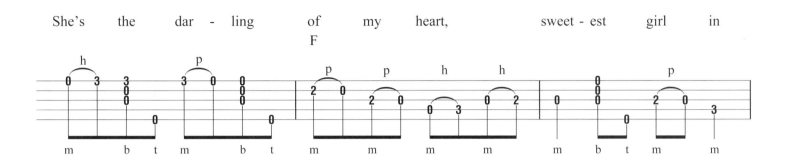

|1.-4. |5.

⊕ Coda

D.C. al Coda

town.   mine.   way.

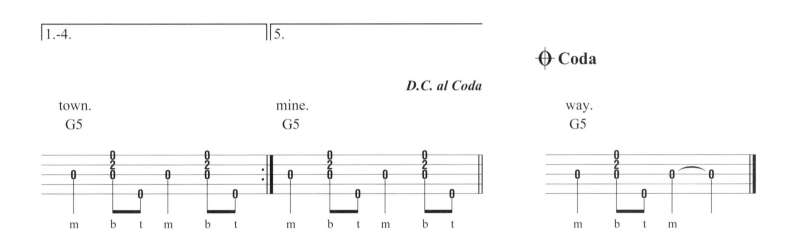

Additional Lyrics

2. I wish I had a big fine horse, and corn to feed him on,
   And Shady Grove to stay at home, and feed him while I'm gone.

3. Went to see my Shady Grove, she was standing at the door.
   Her shoes and stockings in her hand, and her bare feet on the floor.

4. When I was a little boy, I wanted a Barlow knife,
   And now I want little Shady Grove to say she'll be my wife.

5. A kiss from pretty little Shady Grove is sweet as brandy wine,
   And there ain't no girl in this old world that's prettier than mine.

This Land Is Your Land

Words and Music by Woody Guthrie

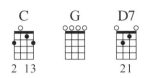

G tuning:
(5th-1st) G-D-G-B-D

Key of G

Moderately, in 2

Verse

1. This land is your land, this land is my land,
walk - ing that rib-bon of high - way,

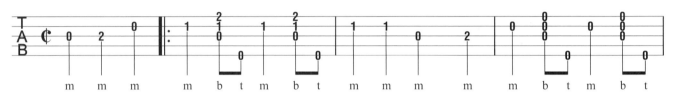

from Cal - i - for - nia to the New York
I saw a - bove me that end - less

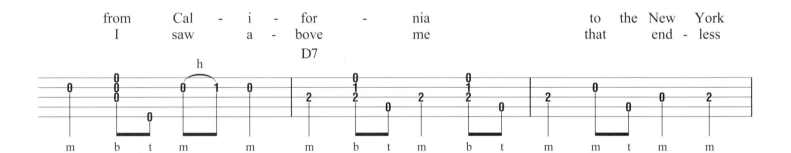

is - land. From the red - wood for - ests
sky - way. I saw be - low me

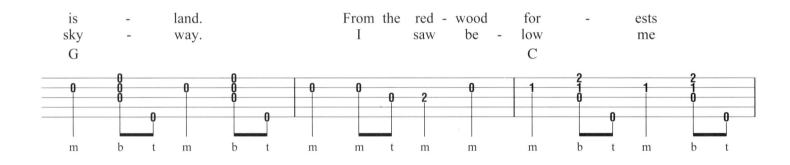

to the Gulf Stream wa - ters, this land was
that gold - en val - ley;

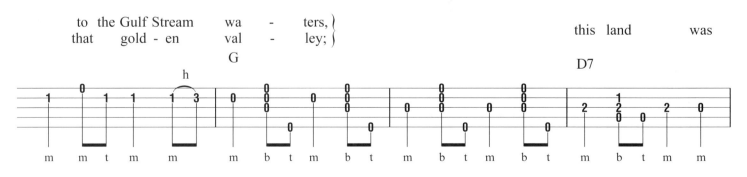

made for   you   and   me.

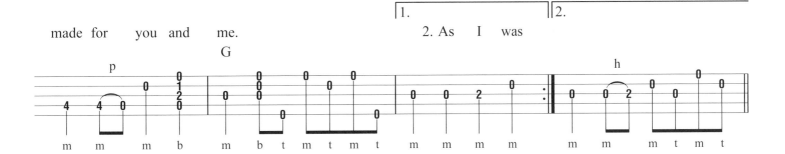

Banjo Break

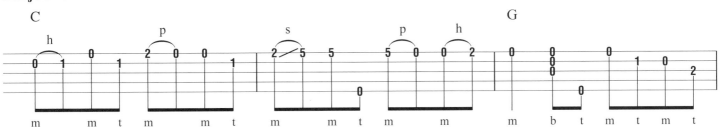

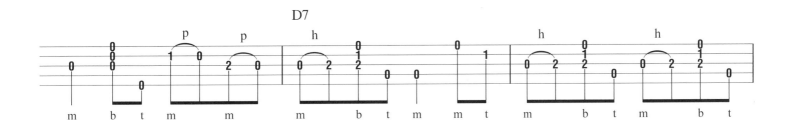

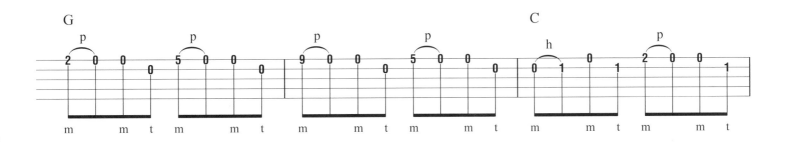

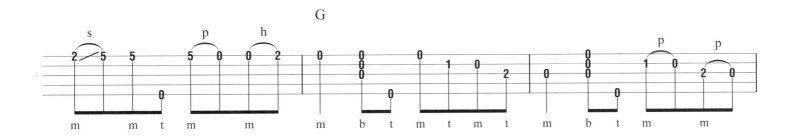

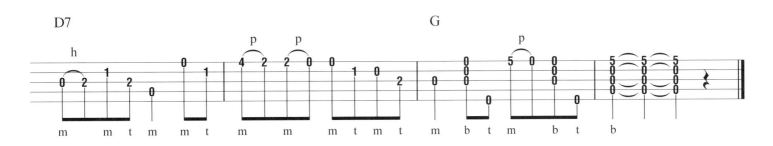

Worried Man Blues

Traditional

G tuning:
(5th-1st) G-D-G-B-D

Key of G

Verse
Moderately

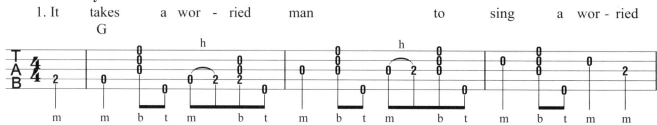

1. It takes a wor - ried man to sing a wor - ried

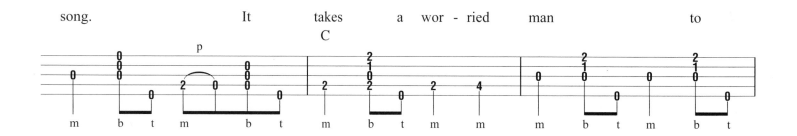

song. It takes a wor - ried man to

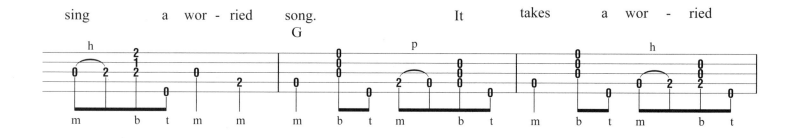

sing a wor - ried song. It takes a wor - ried

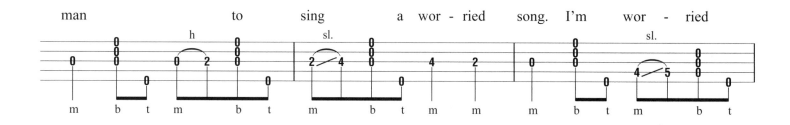

man to sing a wor - ried song. I'm wor - ried

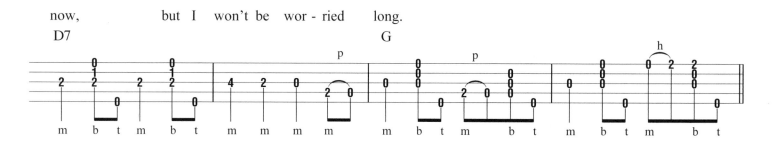

now, but I won't be wor - ried long.

Banjo Break

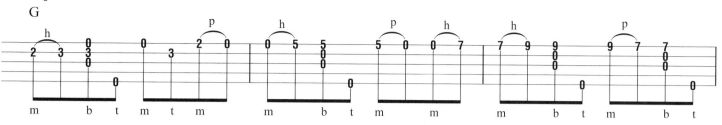

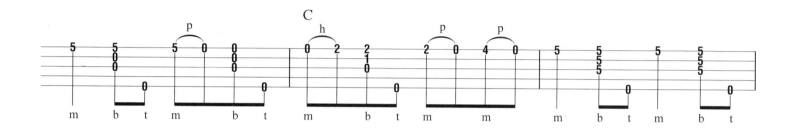

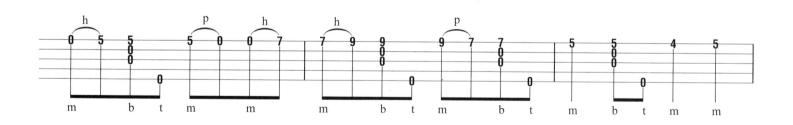

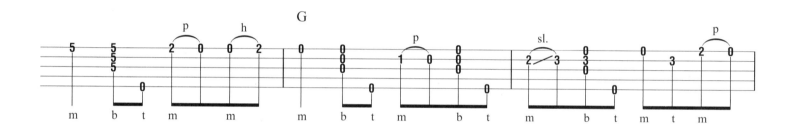

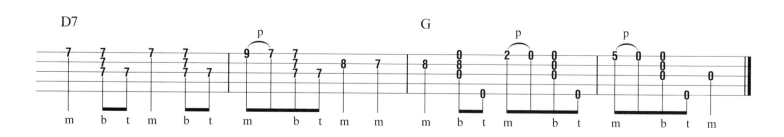

Wind That Shakes the Barley

Traditional Fiddle Tune

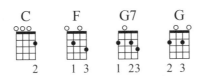

Double C tuning:
(5th–1st) G-C-G-C-D

Key of C

Moderately, in 2

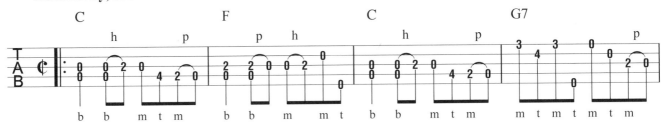

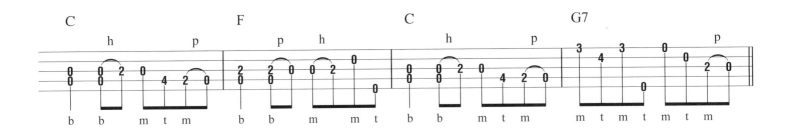

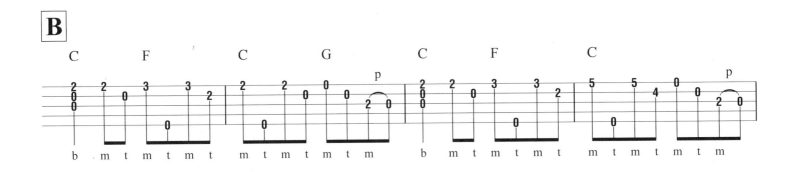

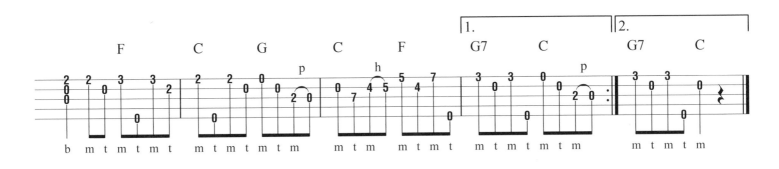

Angeline the Baker

Traditional

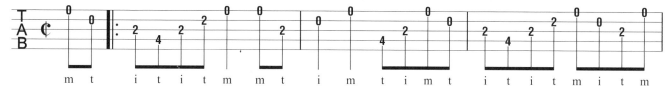

G tuning:
(5th-1st) G-D-G-B-D

Key of D

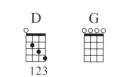

Moderately, in 2

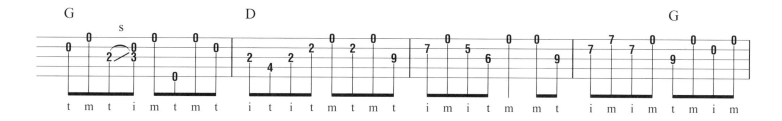

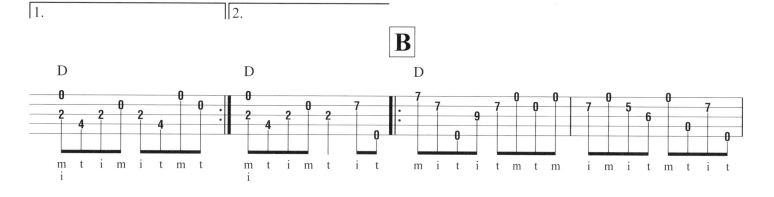

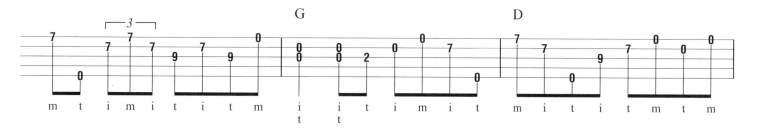

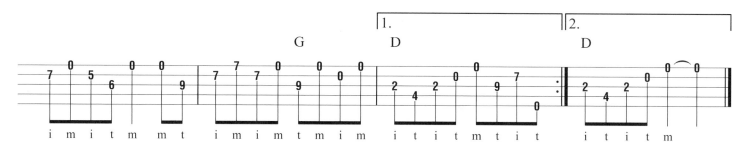

All of Me

Words and Music by Seymour Simons and Gerald Marks

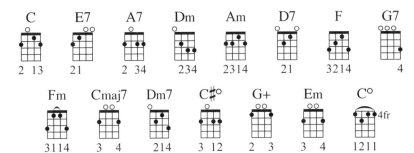

G tuning:
(5th to 1st) G-D-G-B-D

Key of C

Verse

Moderately

All of me, why not take

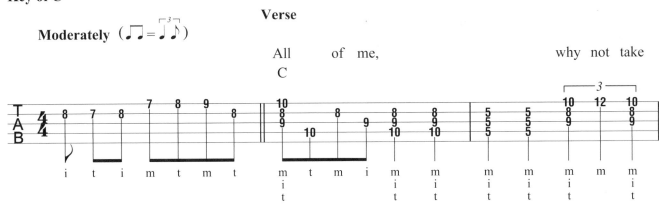

all of me? Can't you see I'm no good with-

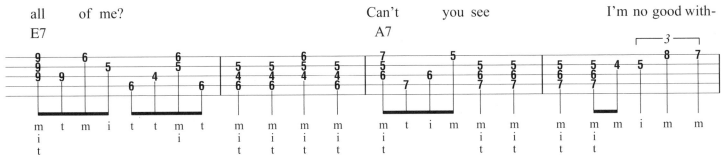

out you? Take my lips, I want to

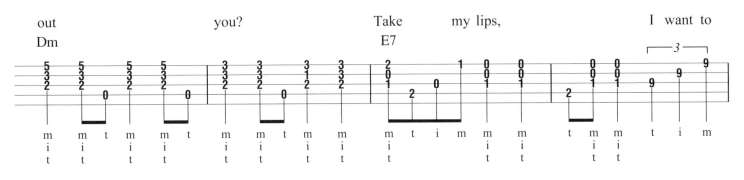

lose them. Take my arms, I'll nev-er

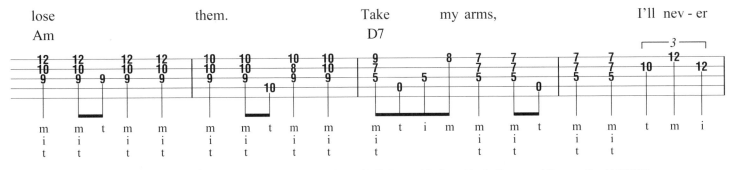

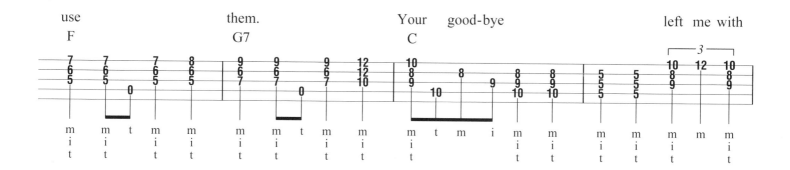

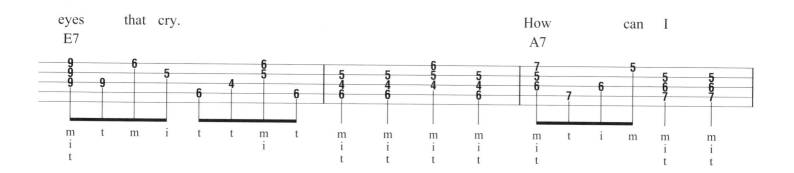

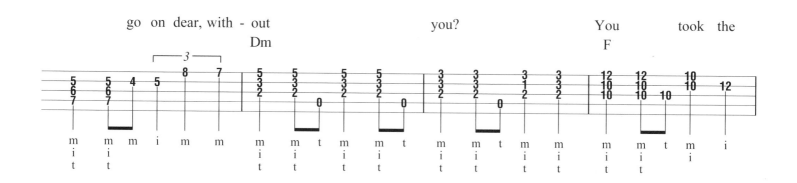

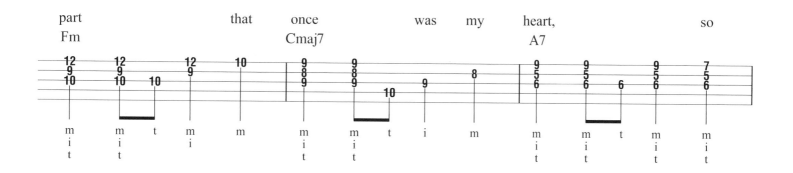

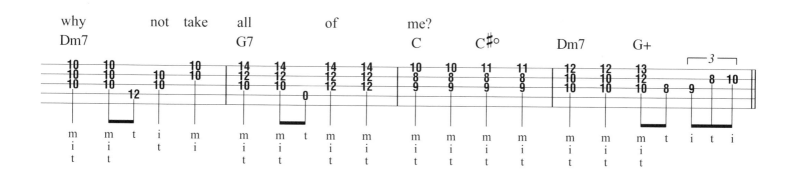

Banjo Break

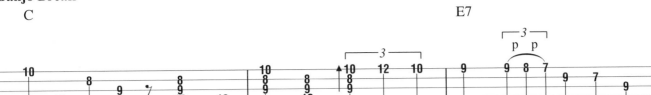

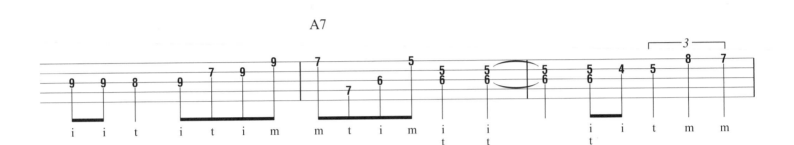

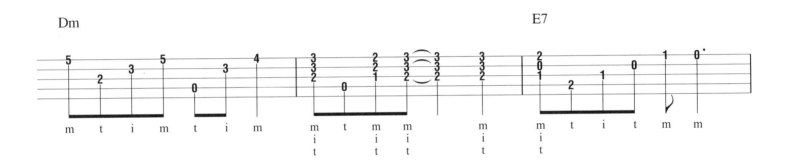

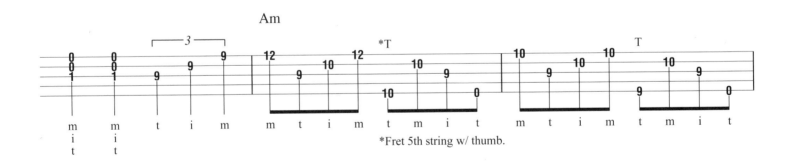

*Fret 5th string w/ thumb.

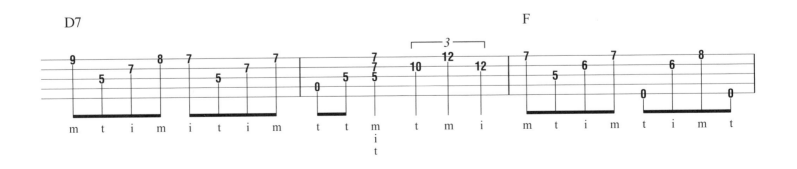

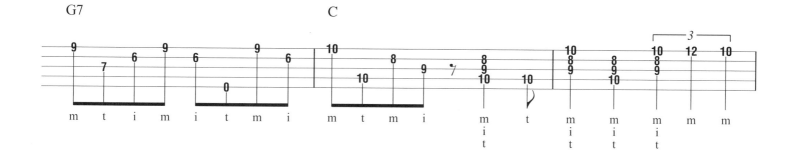

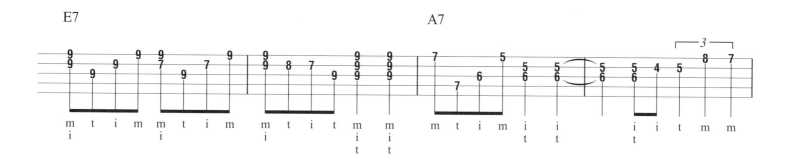

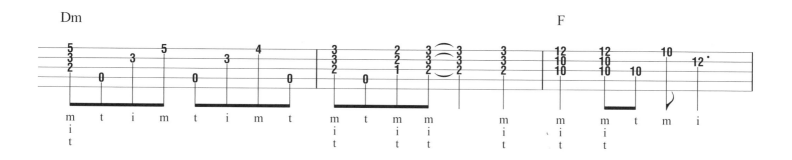

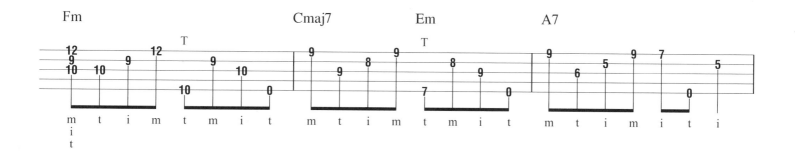

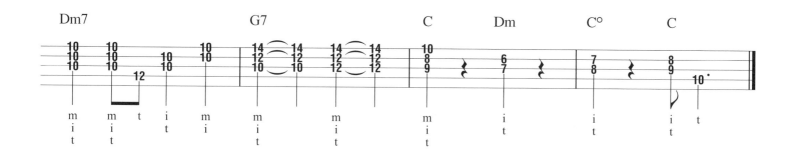

The Beaumont Rag

Traditional

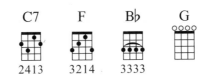

G tuning:
(5th-1st) G-D-G-B-D

Key of C

A

Moderately, in 2

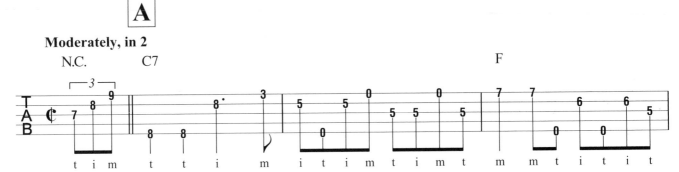

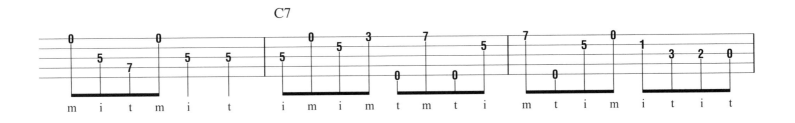

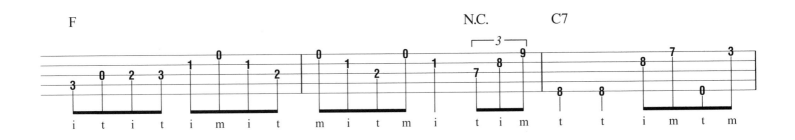

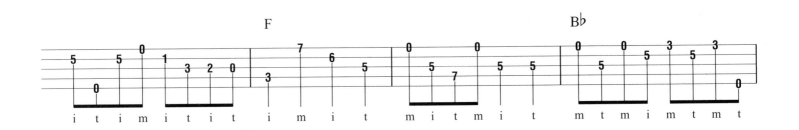

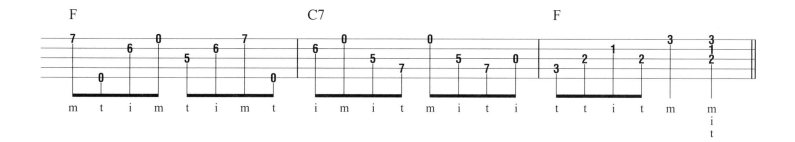

B

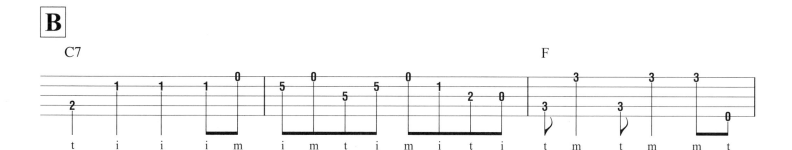

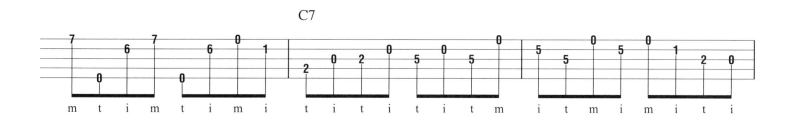

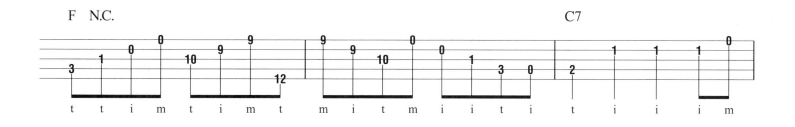

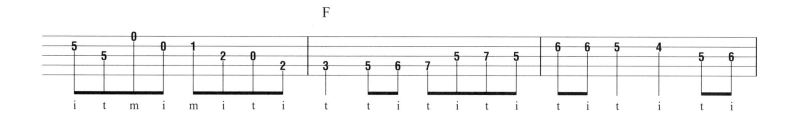

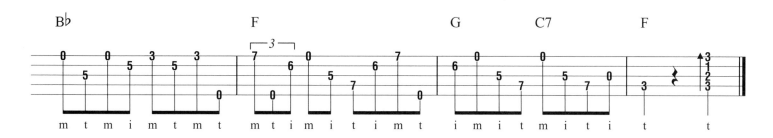

Blue Ridge Cabin Home

Words and Music by Louise Certain and Gladys Stacey

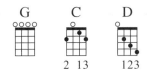

G tuning:
(5th-1st) G-D-G-B-D

Key of D

Banjo Break

Moderately, in 2

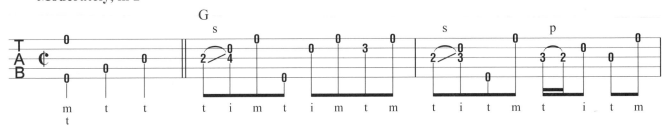

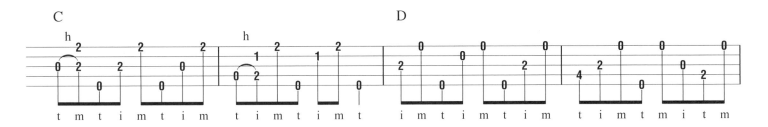

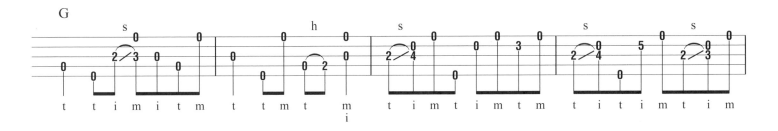

There's a

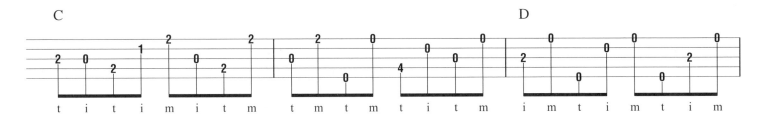

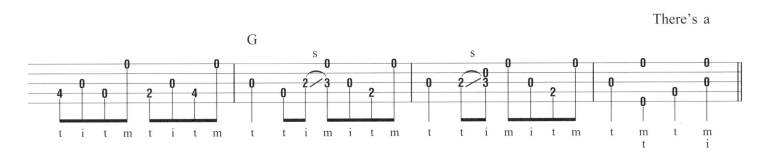

Verse

well - beat - en path on this old moun - tain -

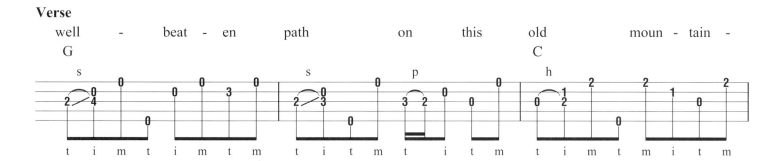

side where I wan - dered when I was a

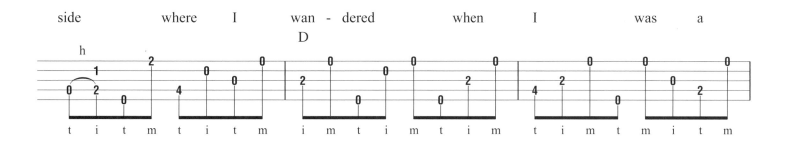

lad. And I wan - dered a -

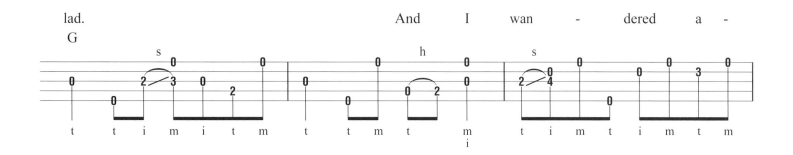

lone to the place I call home in those

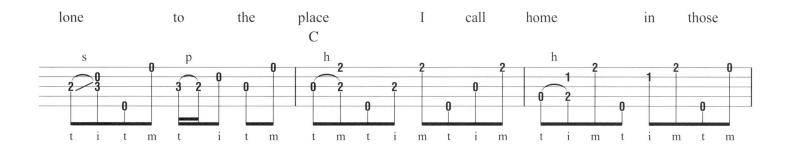

Blue Ridge hills so far a - way. Oh, I

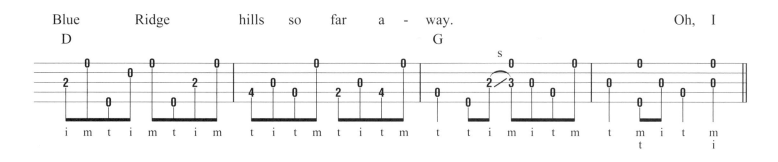

Chorus

love those hills of old Vir - gin - ia.

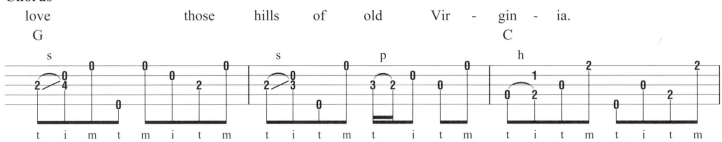

From those Blue Ridge hills I did

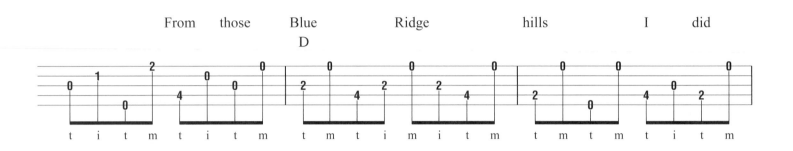

roam. When I die, won't you

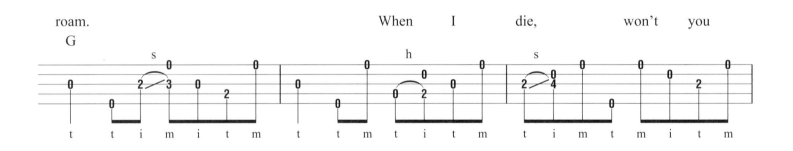

bu - ry me on the moun-tain far a -

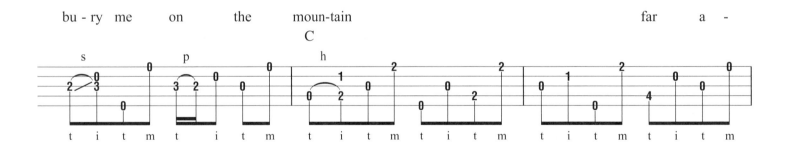

way, near my Blue Ridge moun - tain home?

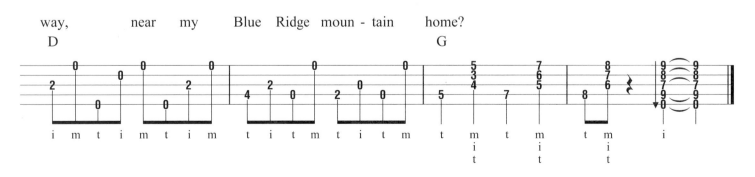

Carolina in the Pines

Words and Music by Michael Martin Murphy

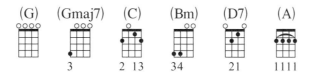

G tuning, capo IV:
(5th-1st) G-D-G-B-D

Key of B

Verse

Moderately

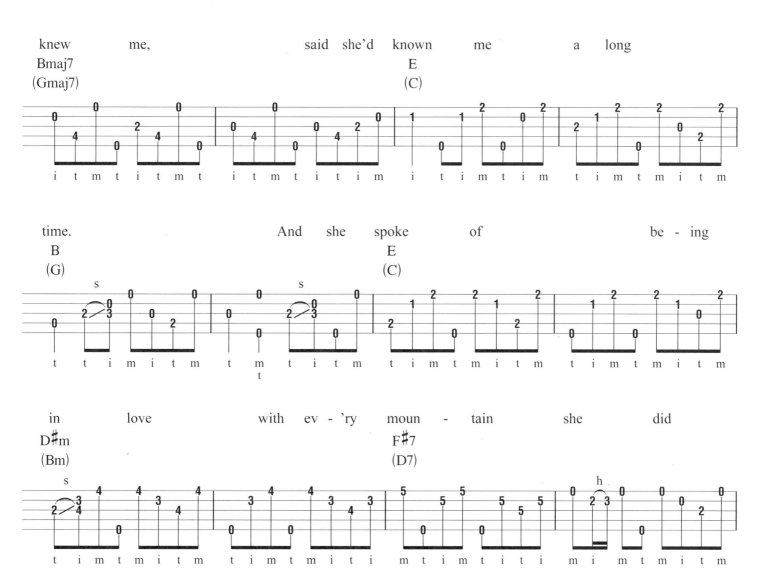

*Symbols in parentheses represent chord names respective to capoed banjo.
Symbols above reflect actual sounding chords. Capoed fret is "0" in tab.

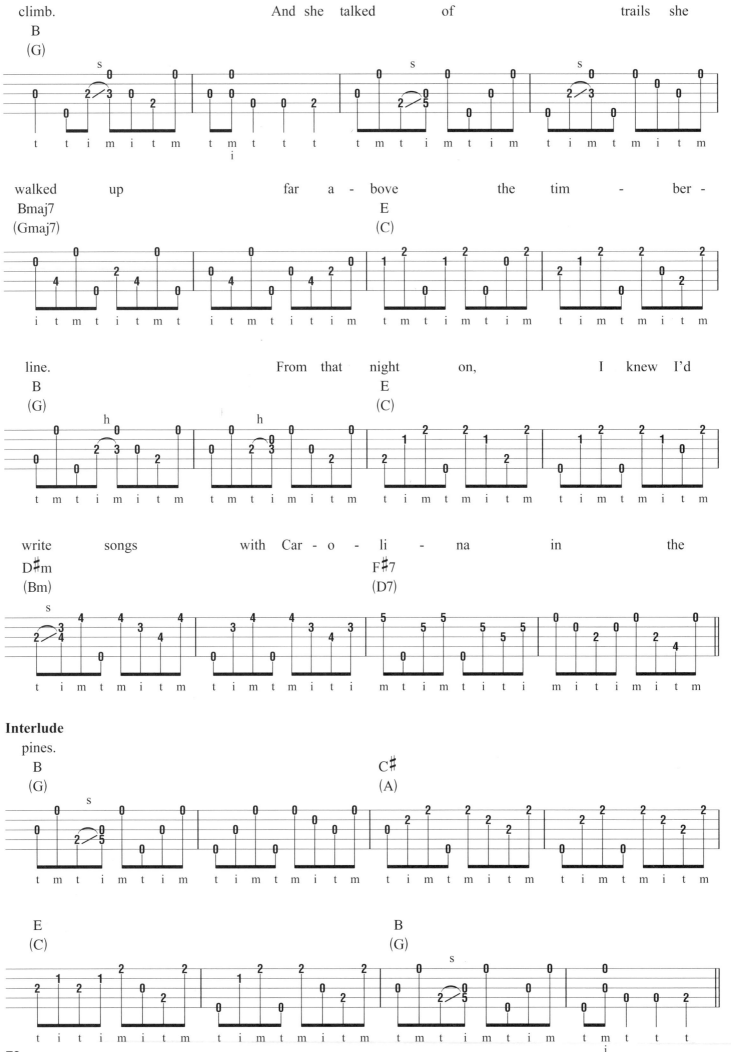

Interlude

Banjo Break

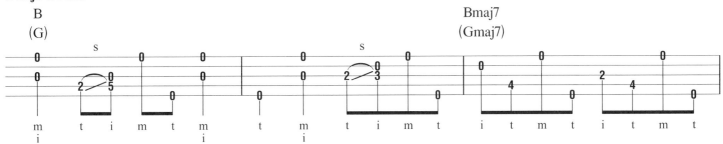

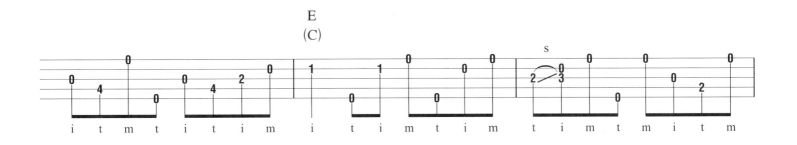

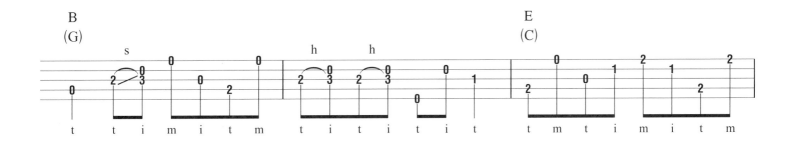

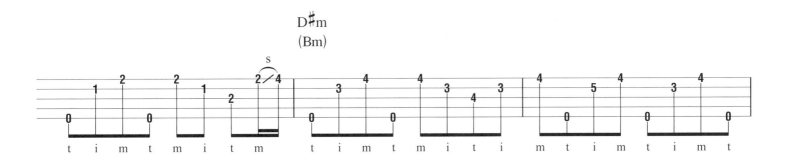

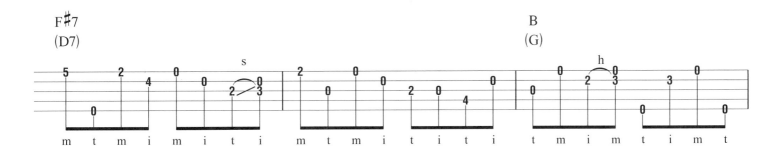

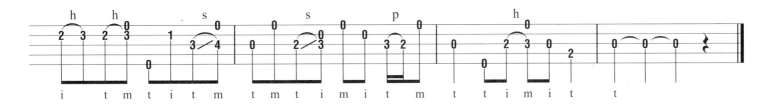

Arkansas Traveler

Southern American Folksong

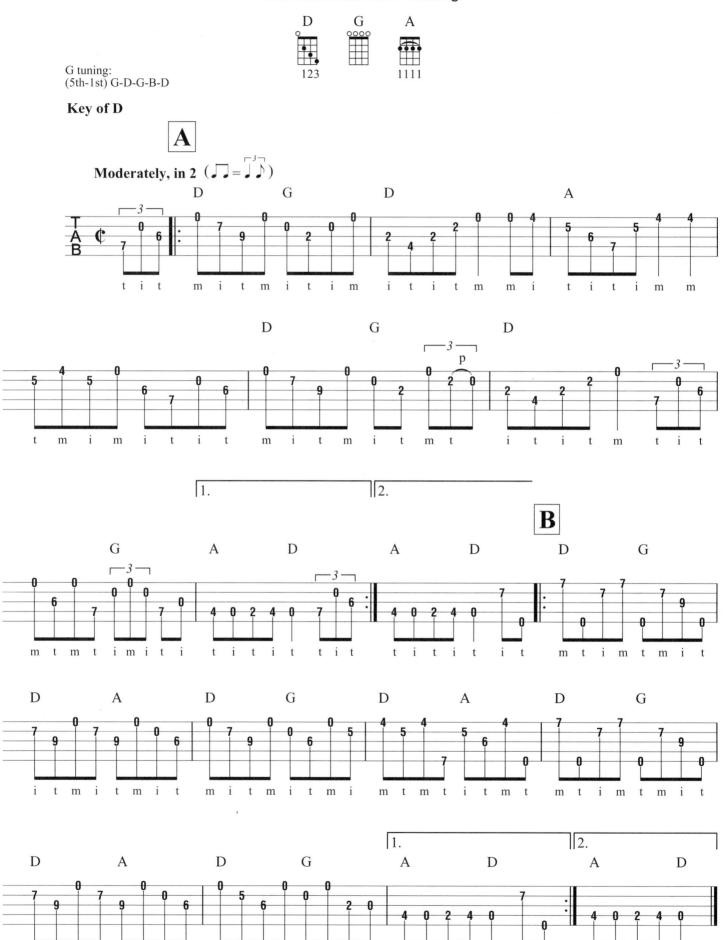

Cripple Creek

American Fiddle Tune

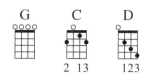

G tuning:
(5th-1st) G-D-G-B-D

Key of G

Moderately fast, in 2

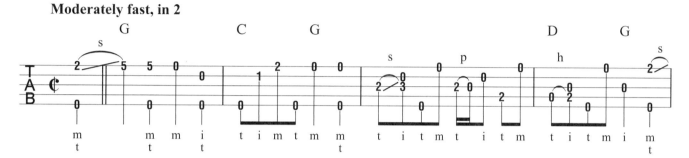

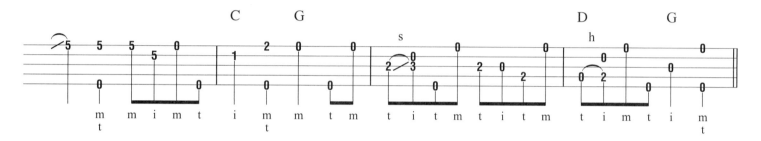

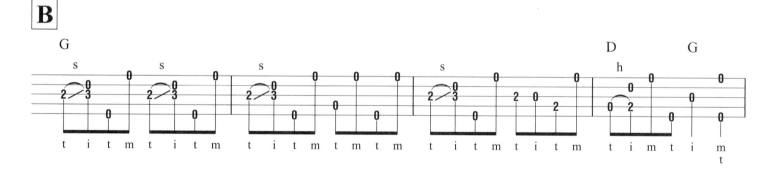

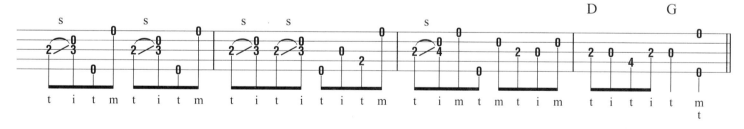

Outro

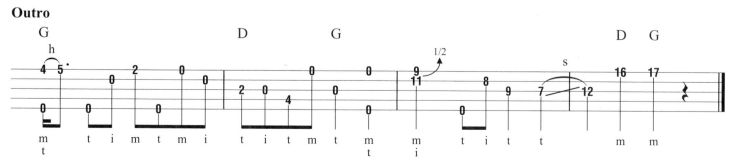

Cuckoo's Nest

Traditional

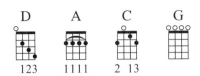

G tuning:
(5th-1st) G-D-G-B-D

Key of D

Intro

Moderately, in 2

N.C.

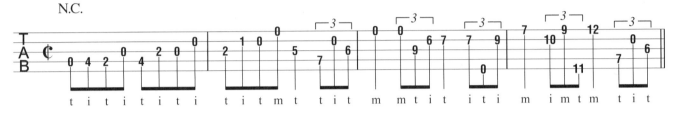

A

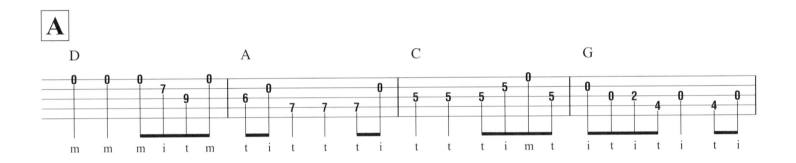

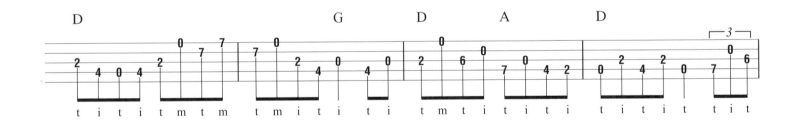

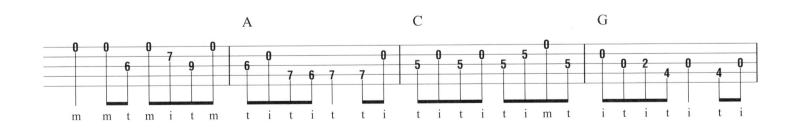

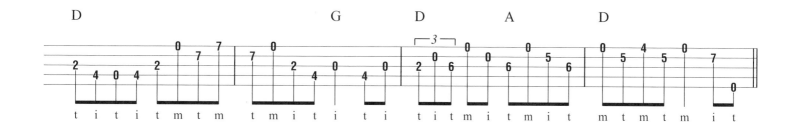

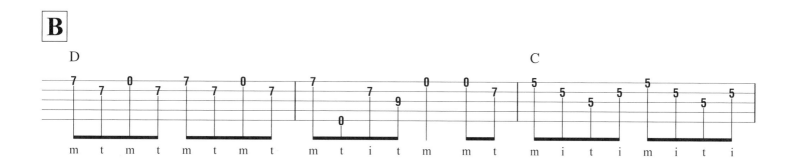

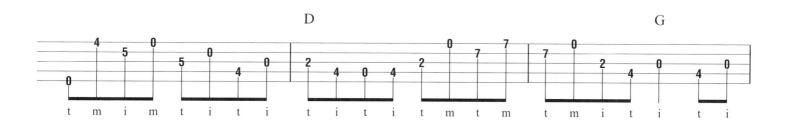

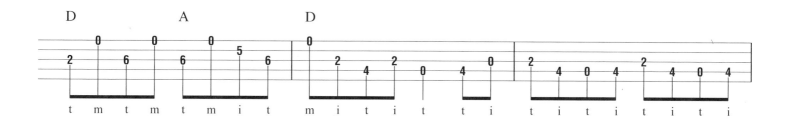

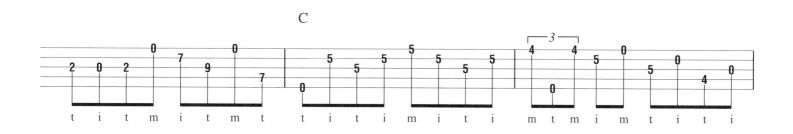

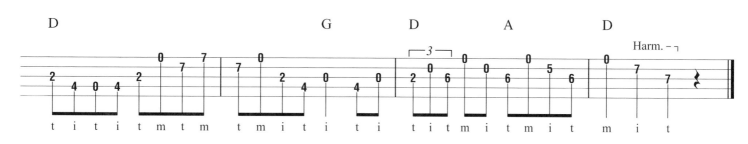

Danny Boy

Words by Frederick Edward Weatherly
Traditional Irish Folk Melody

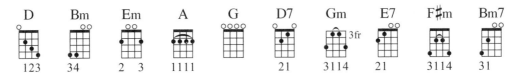

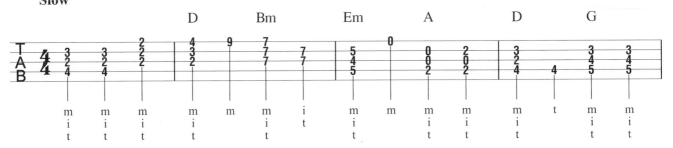

G tuning:
(5th-1st) G-D-G-B-D

Key of D

Intro

Slow

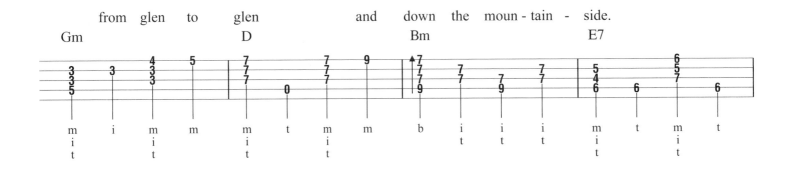

Verse

Oh, Dan - ny Boy, the pipes, the pipes are call - ing

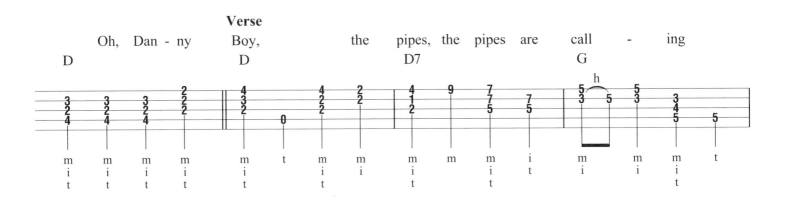

from glen to glen and down the moun - tain - side.

The sum - mer's gone and all the ro - ses dy - ing.

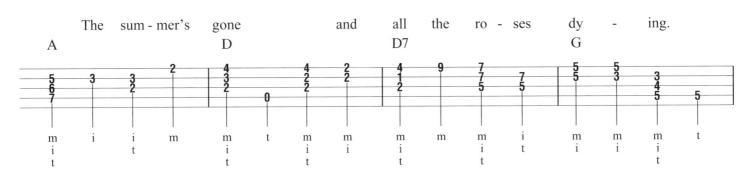

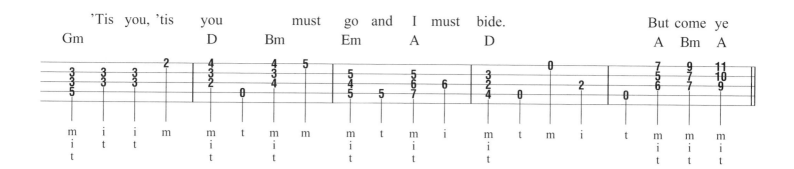

Chorus

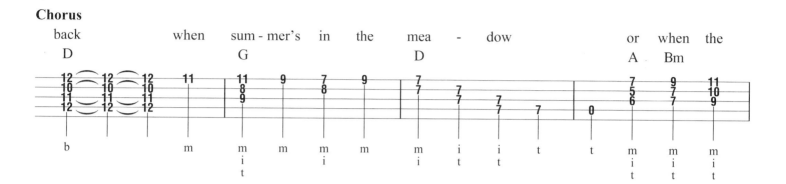

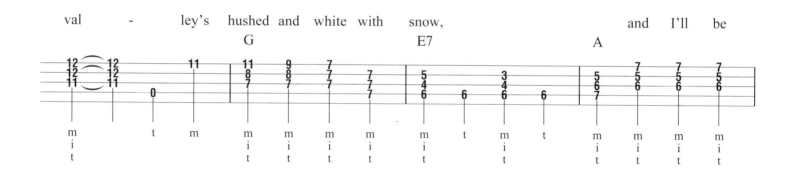

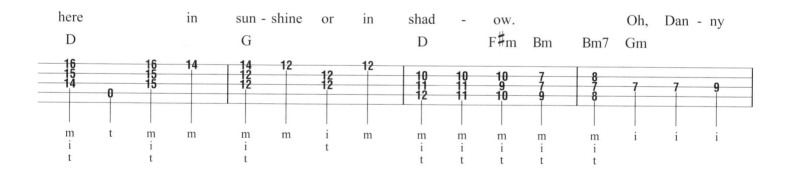

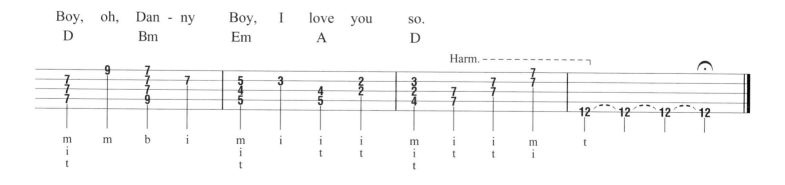

Dark Hollow

Words and Music by Bill Browning

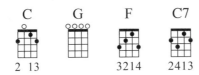

G tuning:
(5th-1st) G-D-G-B-D

Key of C

Verse

Moderately, in 2

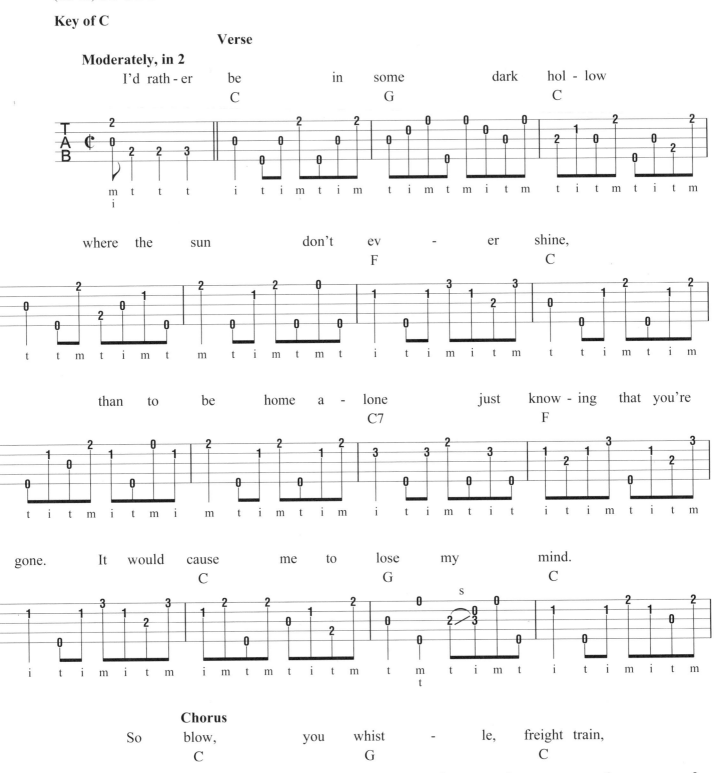

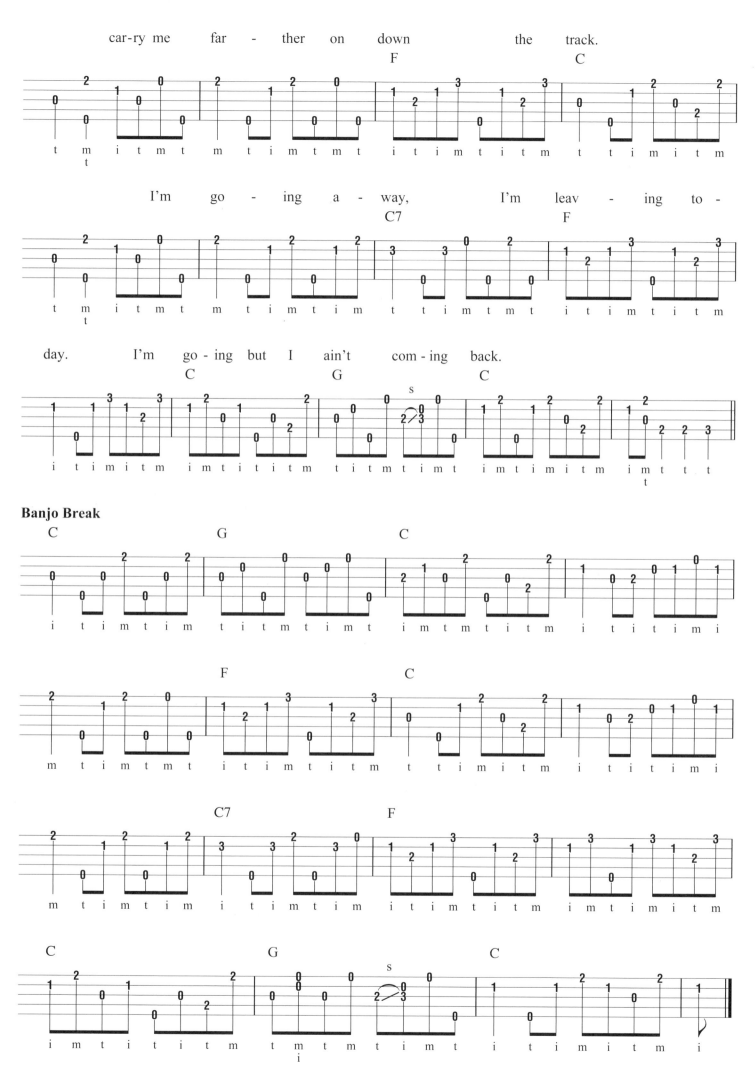

Daley's Reel

Traditional

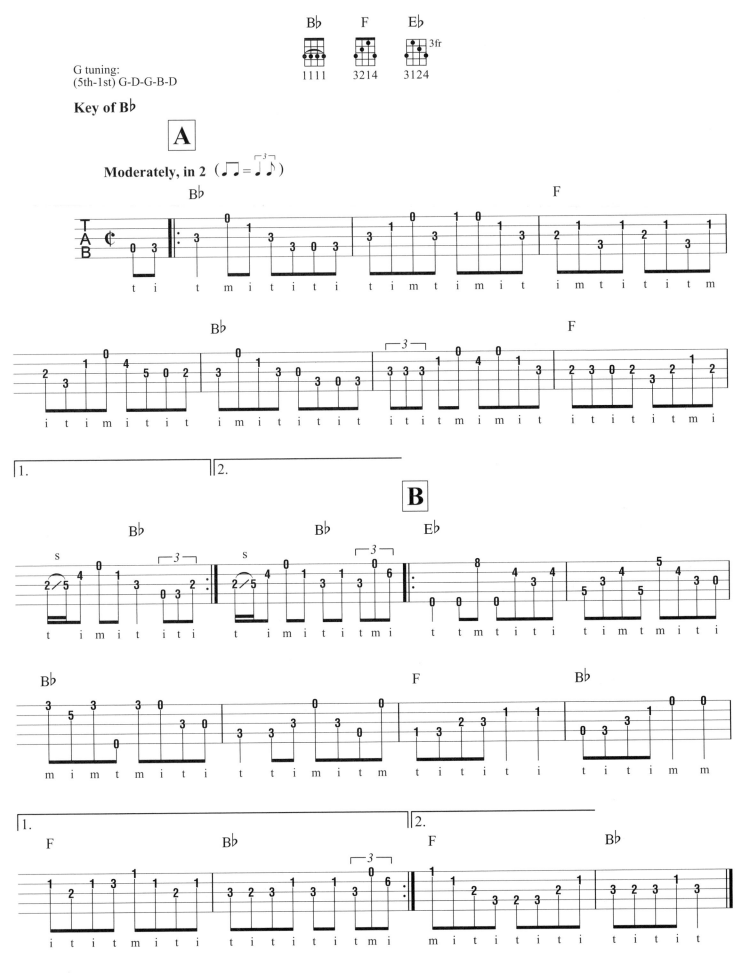

G tuning:
(5th-1st) G-D-G-B-D

Key of B♭

Foggy Mountain Breakdown

By Earl Scruggs

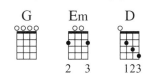

G tuning:
(5th-1st) G-D-G-B-D

Key of G

Moderately fast, in 2

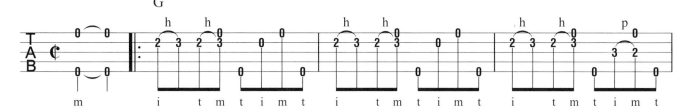

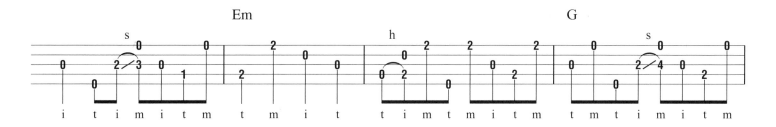

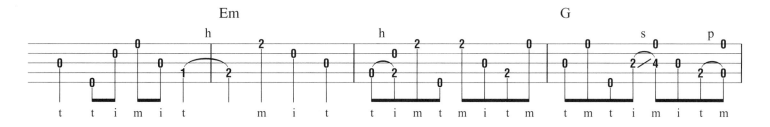

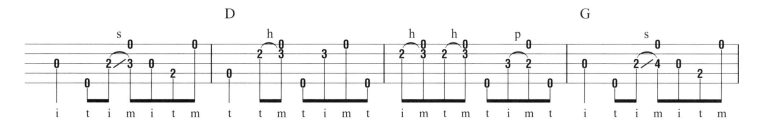

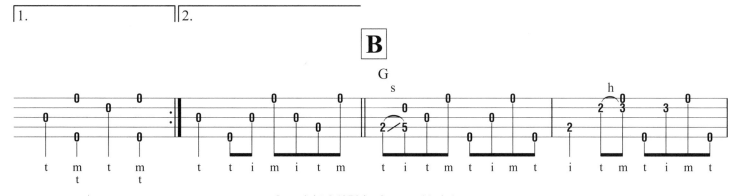

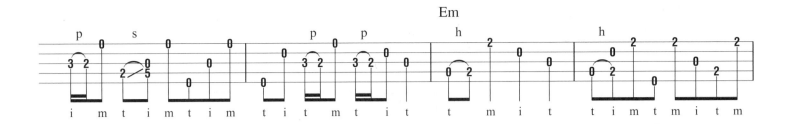

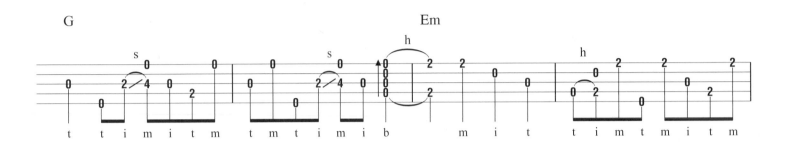

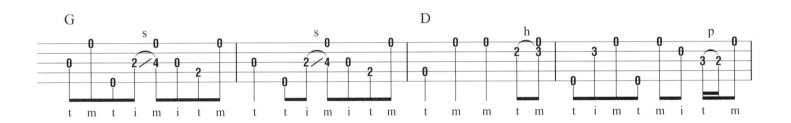

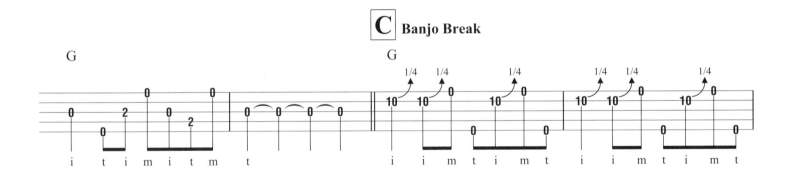

C Banjo Break

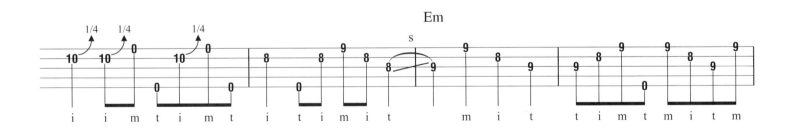

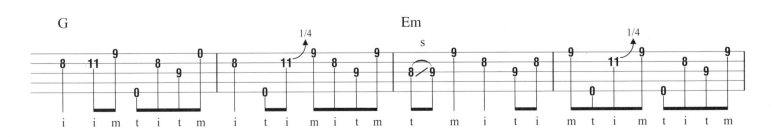

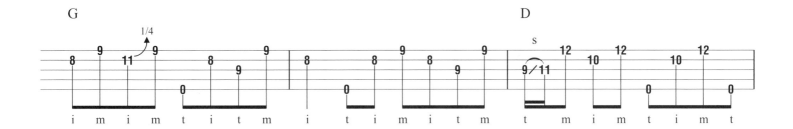

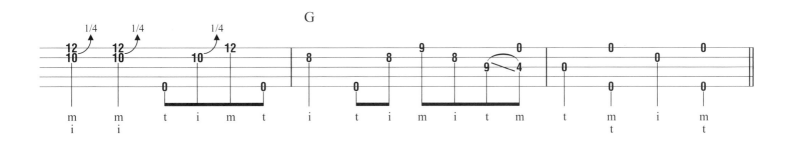

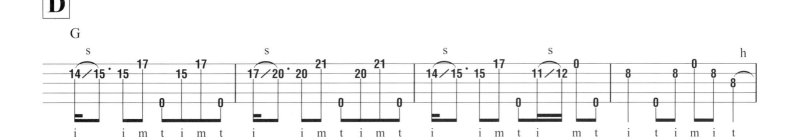

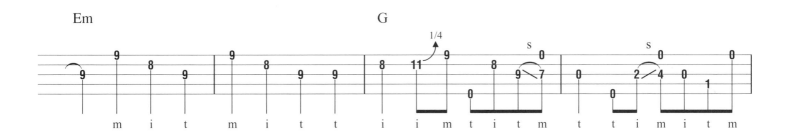

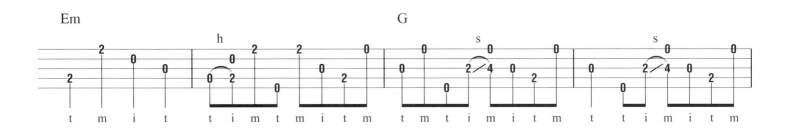

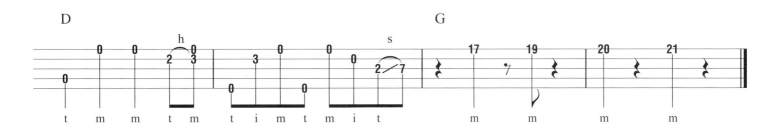

Hey, Good Lookin'

Words and Music by Hank Williams

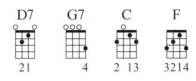

G tuning:
(5th-1st) G-D-G-B-D

Key of C

Intro
Moderately

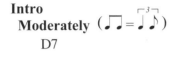

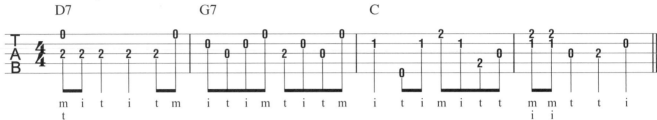

Verse

1. Hey,   good   look-in',   what   ya got   cook-in'?

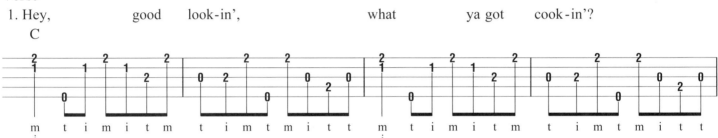

How's a-bout cook-in'   some-thin' up   with   me?

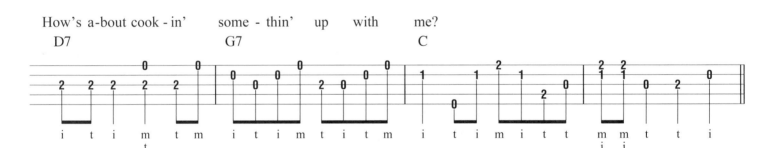

Verse

2. Hey,   sweet   ba-by,   don't   you think   may-be

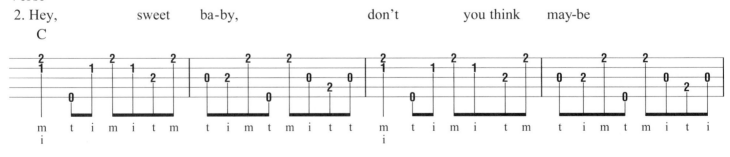

we could find us a brand new rec-i-pe?   I got a

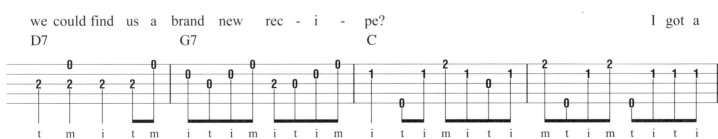

Bridge

hot rod Ford and a two dol - lar bill, and I know a spot right o - ver the hill.

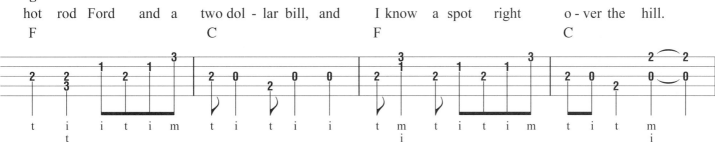

There's so-da pop and the danc-in's free, so if you wan-na have fun, come a - long with me. 3. Say,

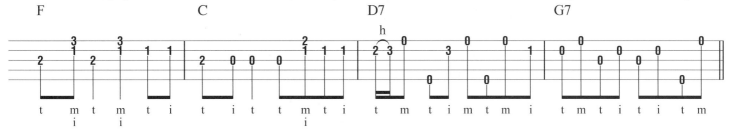

Verse

hey, good look-in', what ya got cook-in'?

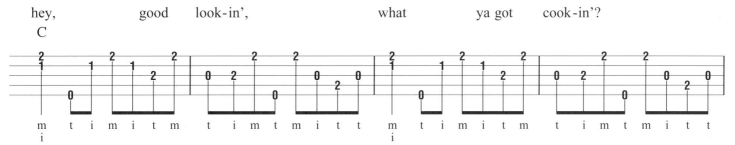

how's a-bout cook - in' some - thin' up with me?

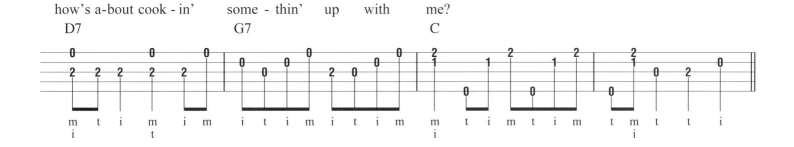

Banjo Break

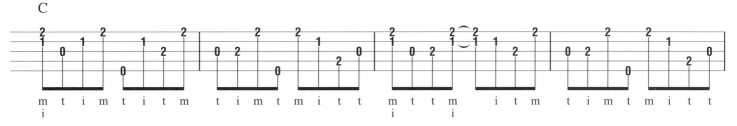

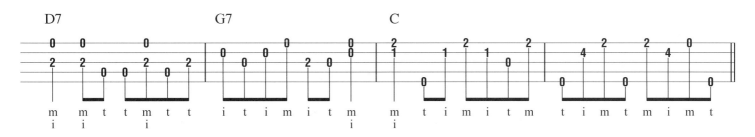

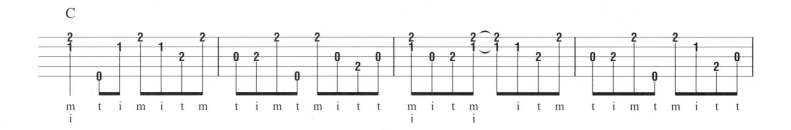

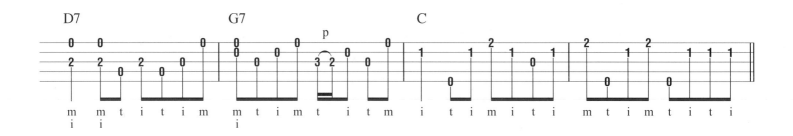

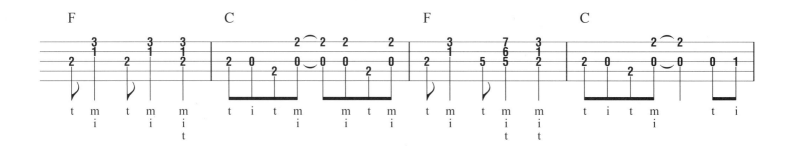

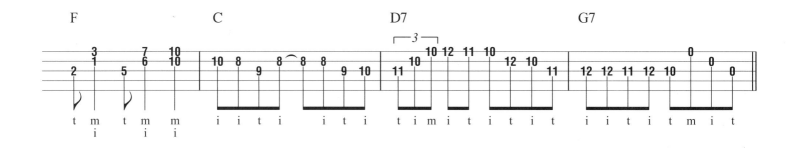

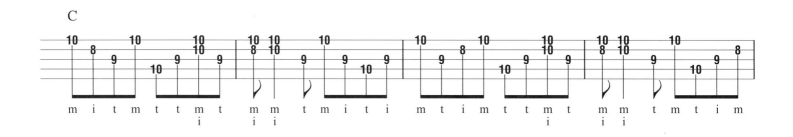

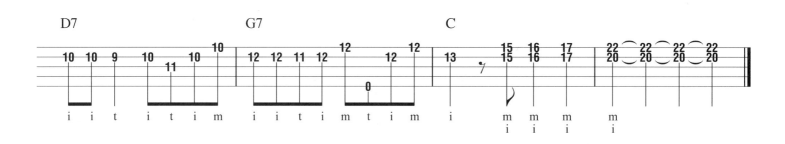

I'll Fly Away

Words and Music by Albert E. Brumley

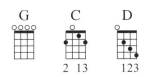

G tuning:
(5th-1st) G-D-G-B-D

Key of G

Banjo Break

Moderately, in 2

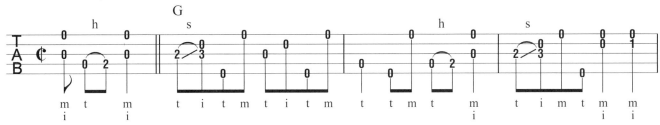

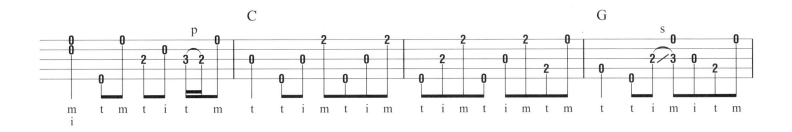

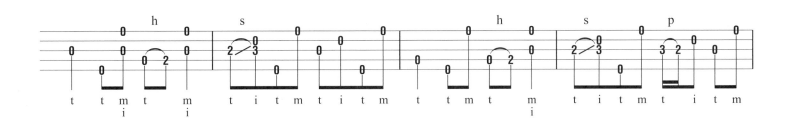

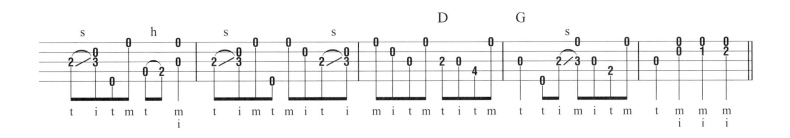

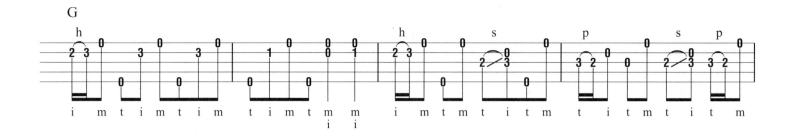

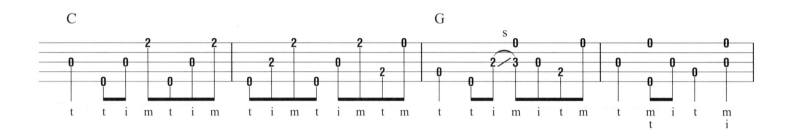

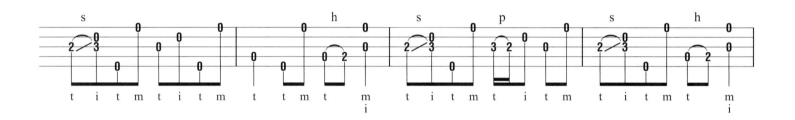

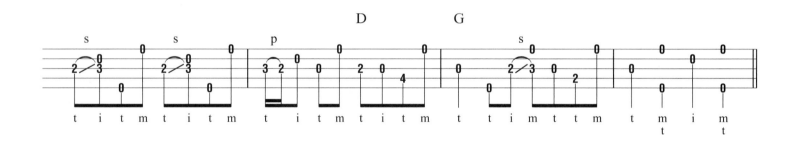

Verse

Some   bright   morn - ing   when   this   life   is   o -   ver,

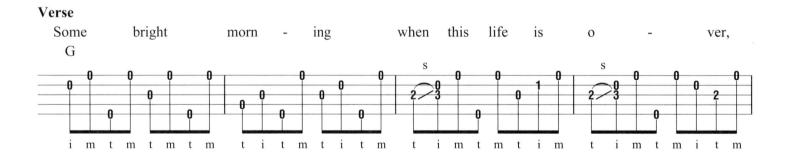

I'll   fly   a - way

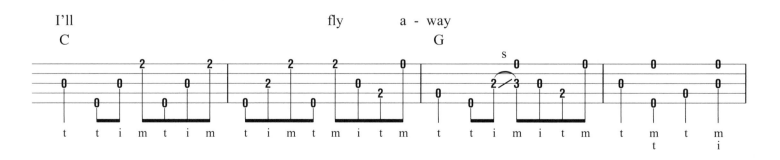

to that home on God's ce - les - tial shore.

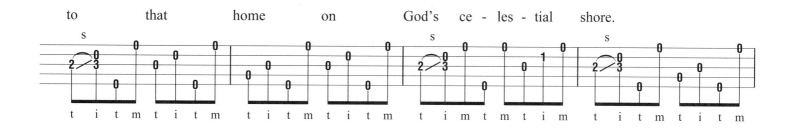

I'll fly a - way.
D   G

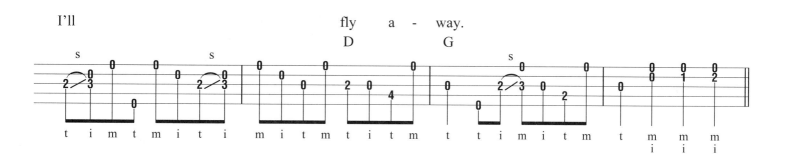

Chorus

I'll fly a - way, oh, glo - ry,
G

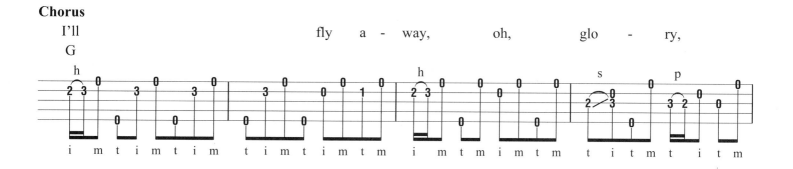

I'll fly a - way.
C   G

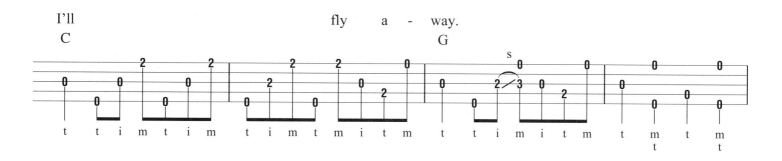

When I die, ha - le - lu - jah by and by,

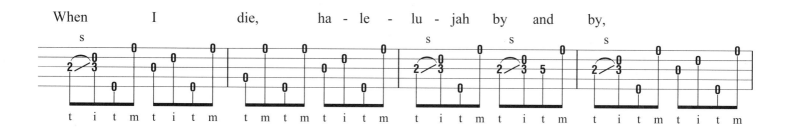

I'll fly a - way.
D   G

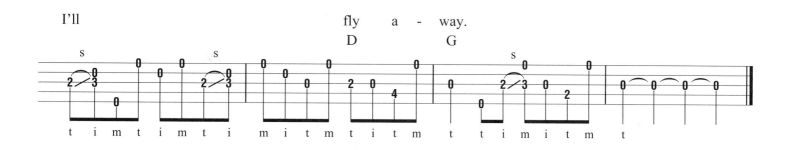

I Am a Man of Constant Sorrow

Words and Music by Carter Stanley

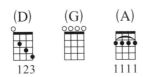

(D)   (G)   (A)

123   1111

Tuning, capo III:
(5th–1st) A-D-G-B-D

Key of F

Verse

Moderately, in 2

1. I   am   a   man
2. For   six long years

F
*(D)

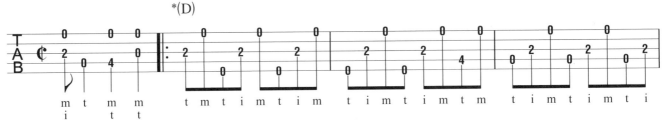

*Symbols in parentheses represent chord names respective to capoed banjo.
Symbols above reflect actual sounding chords. Capoed fret is "0" in tab.

of con - stant sor - row,   I've seen trou -
I've been in   trou - ble,   no pleas - ures here

Bb   C
(G)   (A)

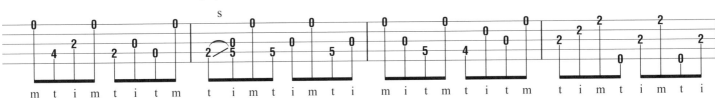

- ble all my days.   I
on earth I found.   For

F
(D)

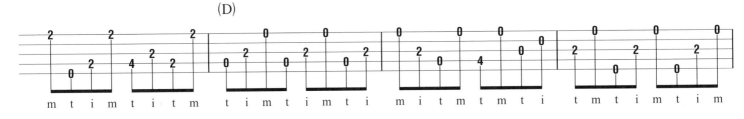

bid fare - well   to old Ken - tuc - ky
in this world   I'm bound to ram - ble,

Bb
(G)

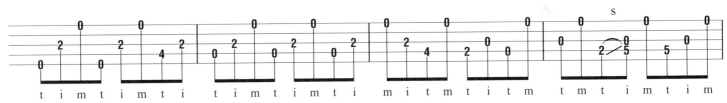

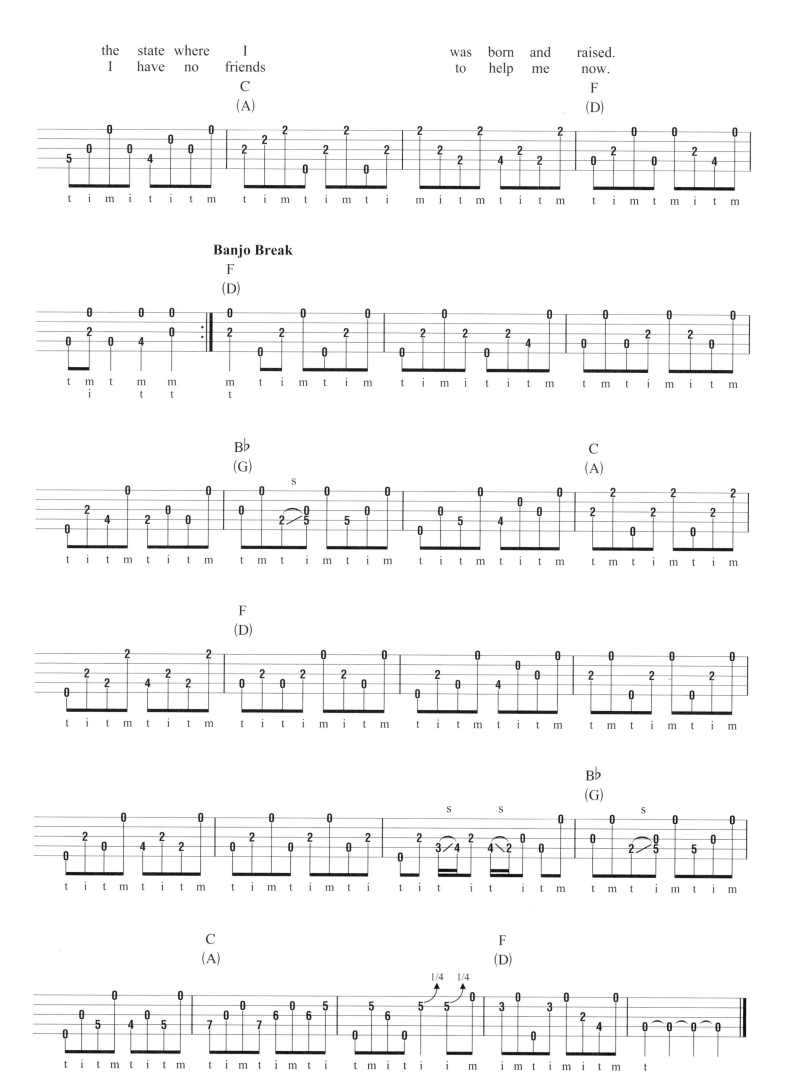

Little Rock Getaway

Music by Joe Sullivan
Words by Carl Sigman

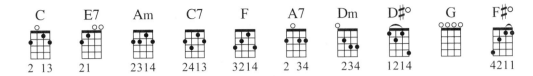

G tuning:
(5th-1st) G-D-G-B-D

Key of G

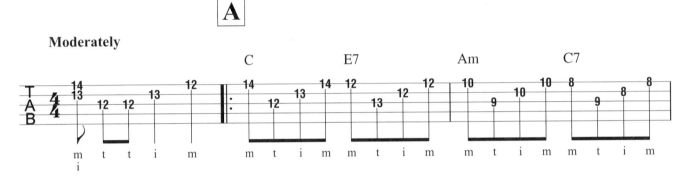

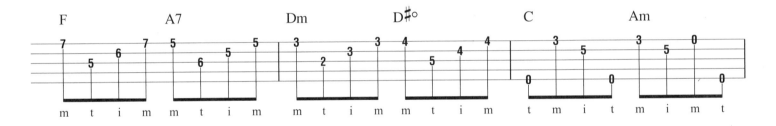

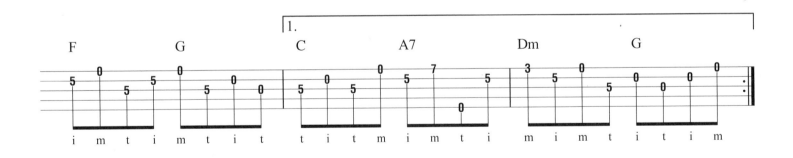

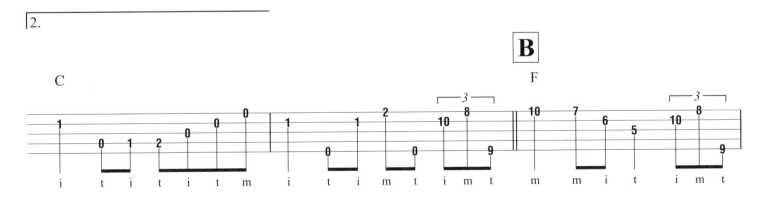

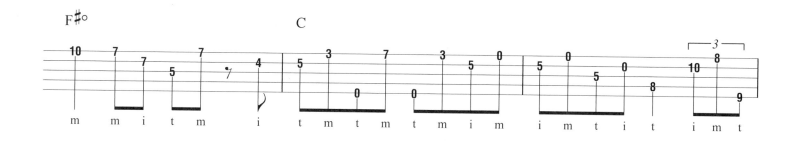

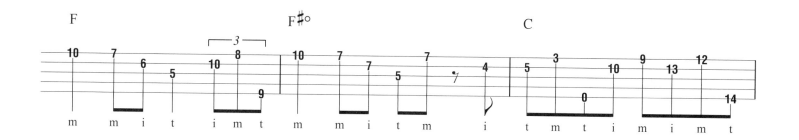

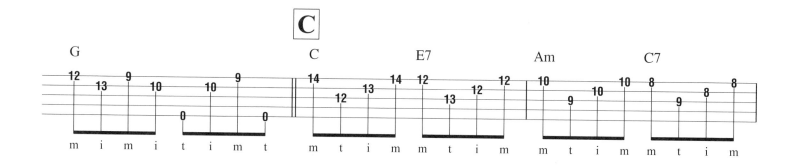

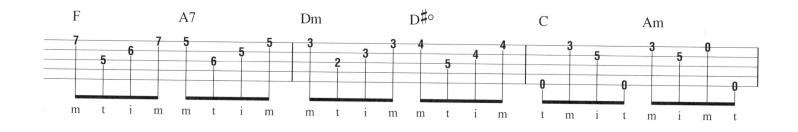

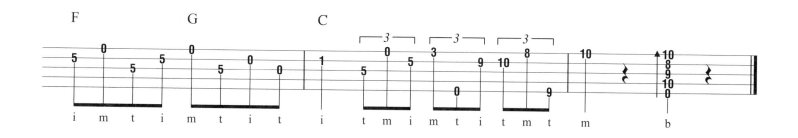

Paradise

Words and Music by John Prine

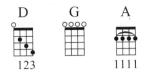

Tuning:
(5th-1st) A-D-G-B-D

Key of D

Banjo Break

Moderately

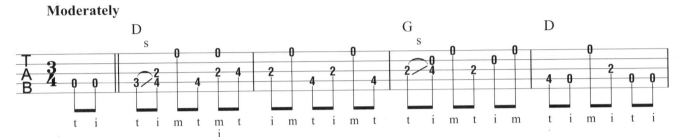

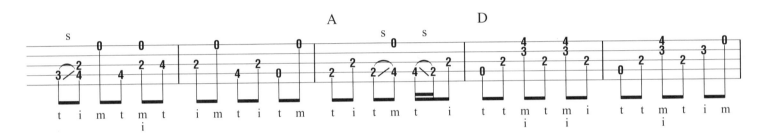

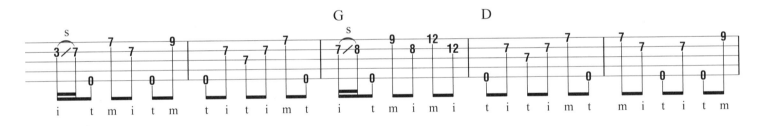

Verse

1. When I was a
   die, let my

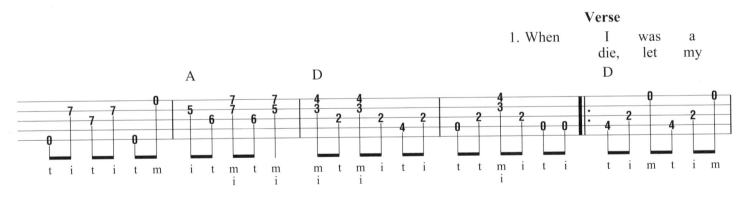

child, my fam-ily would trav-el down to wes-tern Ken-tuc-ky where my
ash-es flow down the Green Riv-er, let my soul roll on up to the

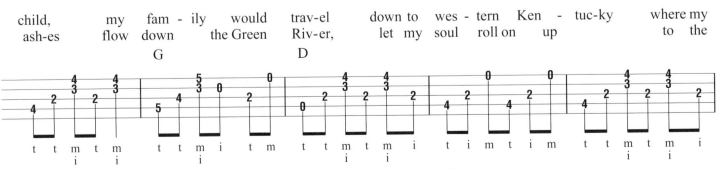

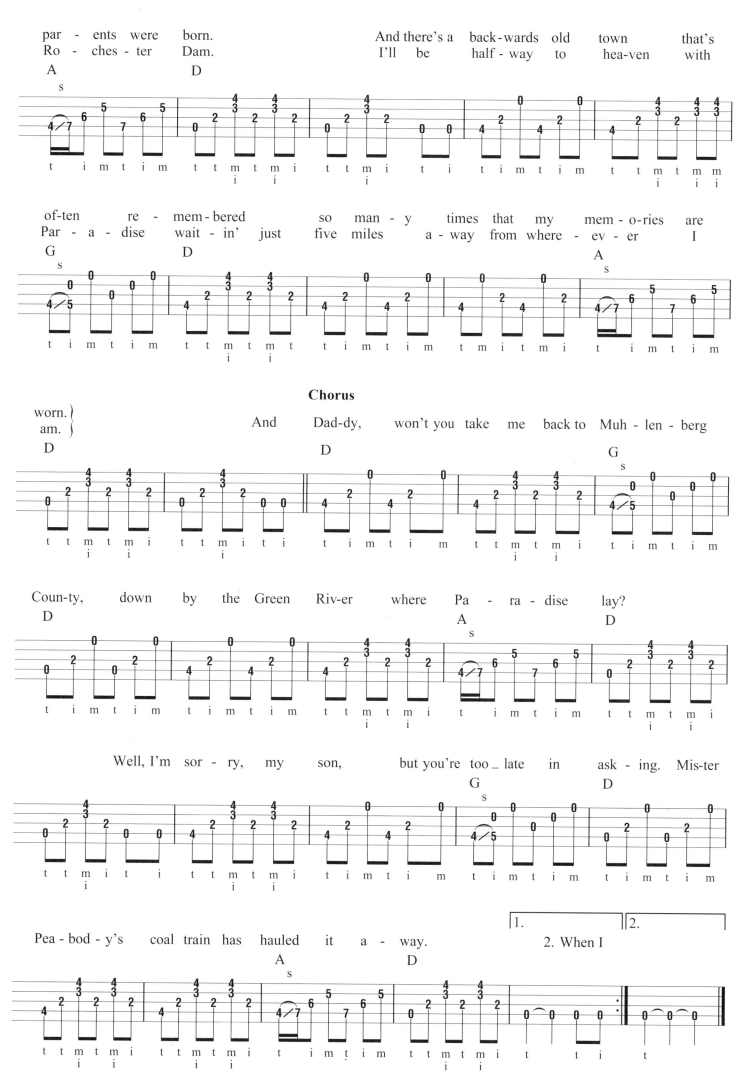

Redwing

Traditional

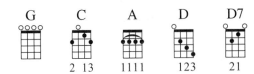

G tuning:
(5th-1st) G-D-G-B-D

Key of G

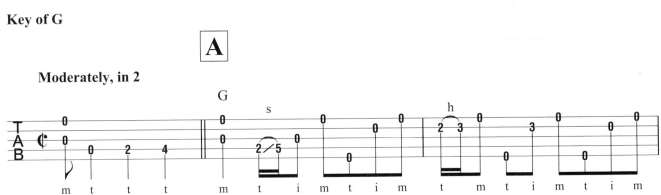

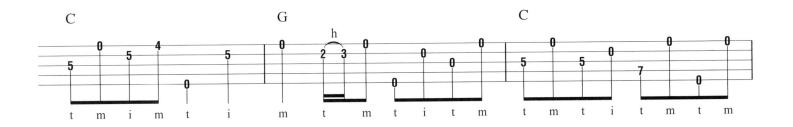

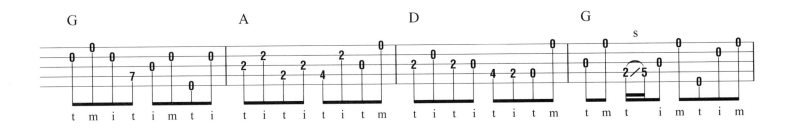

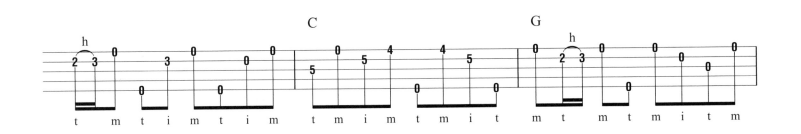

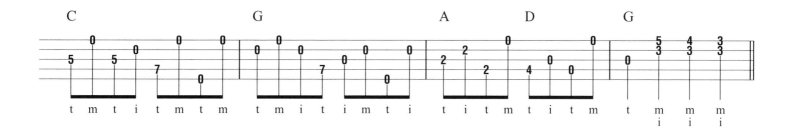

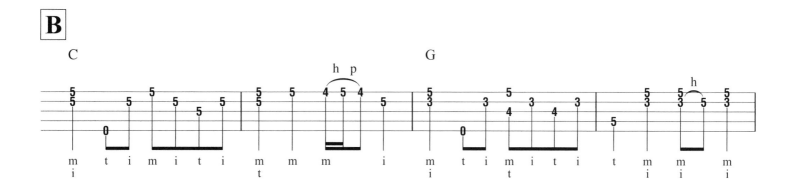

B

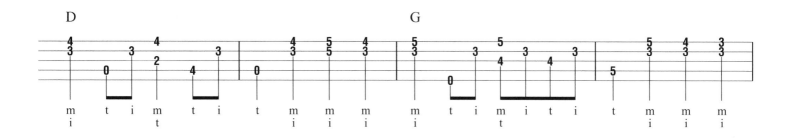

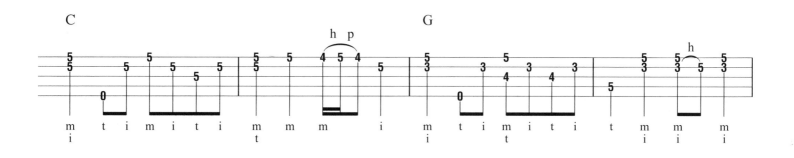

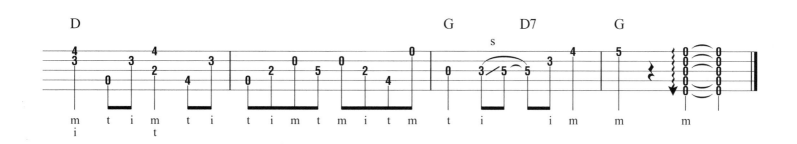

Sitting on Top of the World

Words and Music by Walter Jacobs and Lonnie Carter

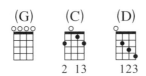

G tuning, capo IV:
(5th-1st) G-D-G-B-D

Key of B

Banjo Break

Moderately

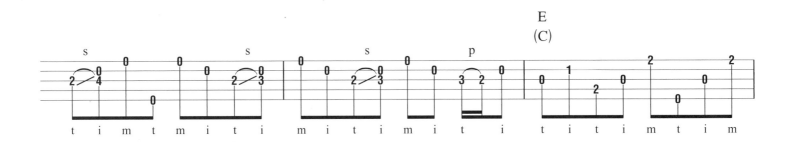

*Symbols in parentheses represent chord names respective to capoed banjo.
Symbols above reflect actual sounding chords. Capoed fret is "0" in tab.

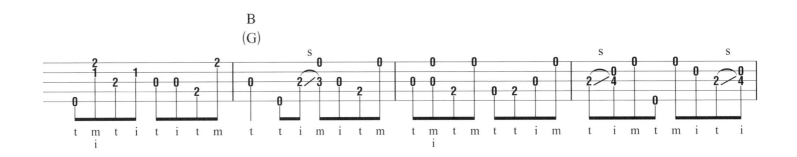

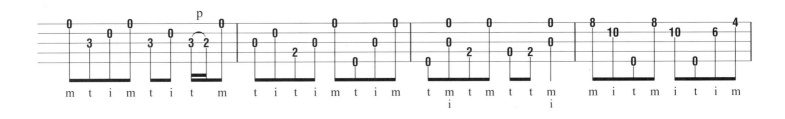

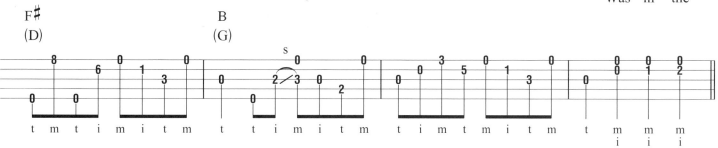

Verse

spring   one sun - ny   day,   my good gal

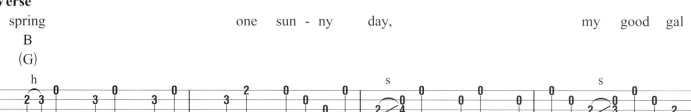

left   me,   she   went a - way.   And now she's

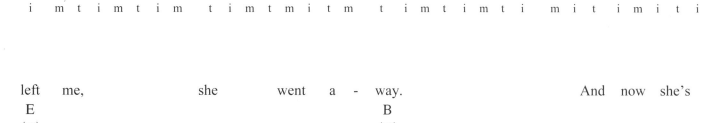

gone,   but   I   don't wor - ry   be - cause I'm

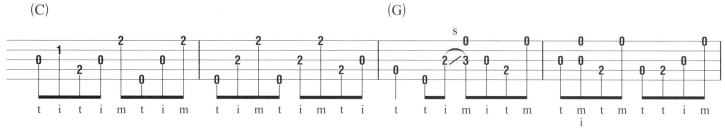

sit - tin'   on   top   of   the   world.

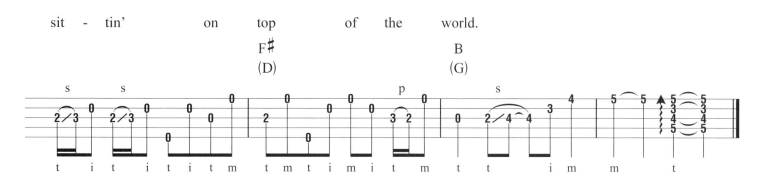

Old Joe Clark

Tennessee Folksong

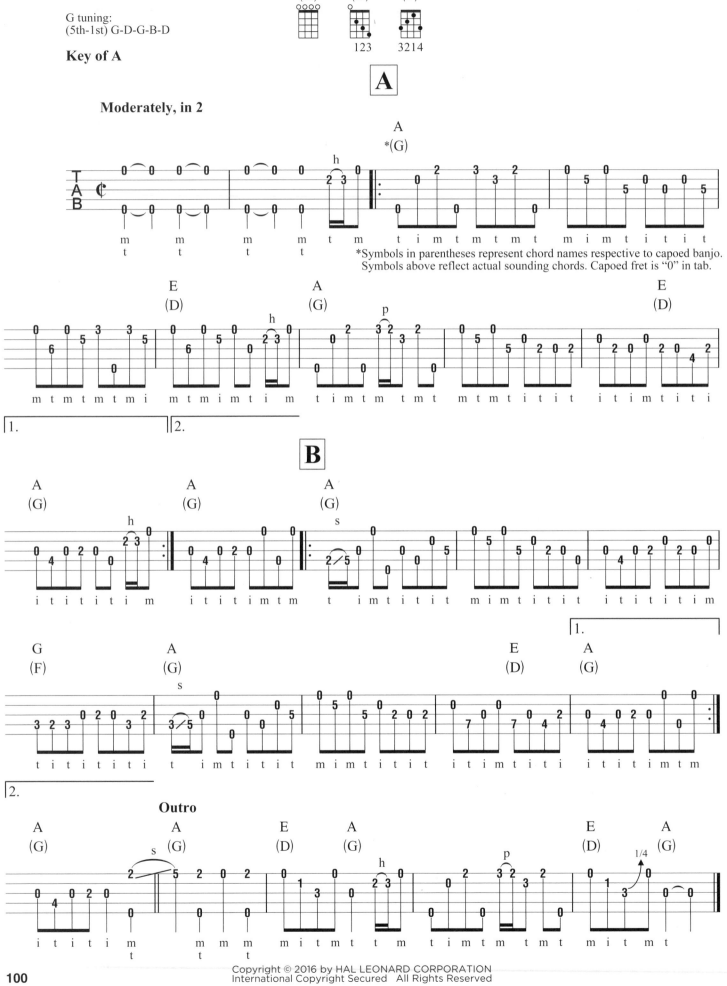

*Symbols in parentheses represent chord names respective to capoed banjo.
Symbols above reflect actual sounding chords. Capoed fret is "0" in tab.

Soldier's Joy

Traditional

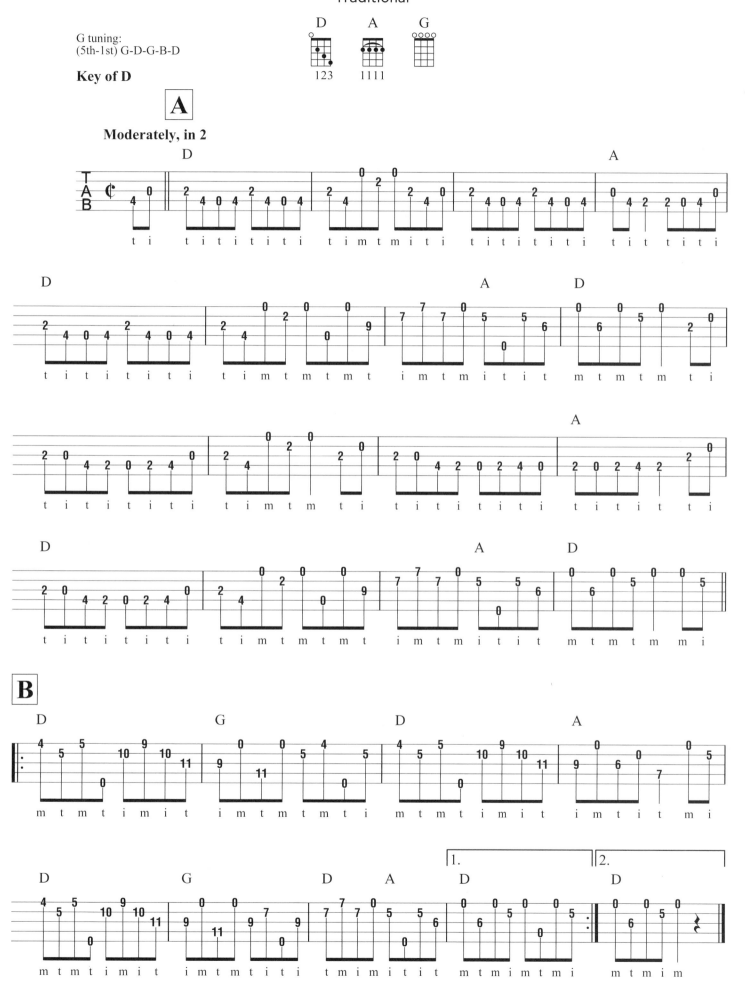

Take Me Home, Country Roads

Words and Music by John Denver, Bill Danoff and Taffy Nivert

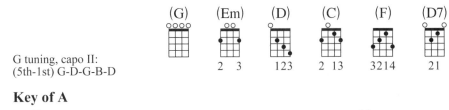

G tuning, capo II:
(5th-1st) G-D-G-B-D

Key of A

Intro

Moderately

Verse

1. Al - most hea - ven,
2. All my mem - 'ries

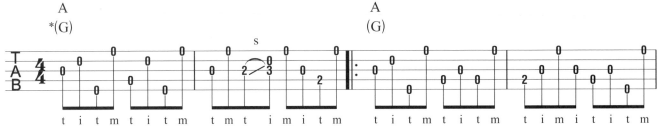

*Symbols in parentheses represent chord names respective to capoed banjo.
Symbols above reflect actual sounding chords. Capoed fret is "0" in tab.

West Vir - gin - ia,   Blue Ridge moun - tains,
gath - er 'round her.   Mi - ner's la - dy,

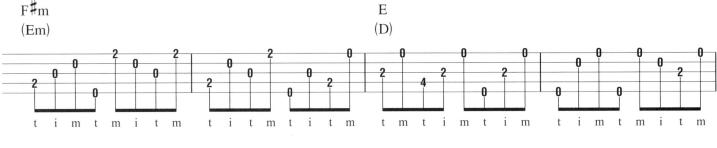

Shen - an - do - ah Riv - er.   Life is
strang - er to blue wa - ter.   Dark and

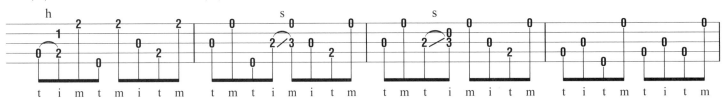

old   there,   old - er   than   the   trees,
dust - y,   paint - ed   on   the   sky,

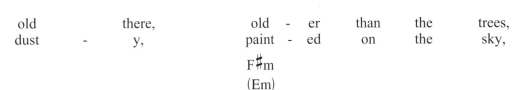

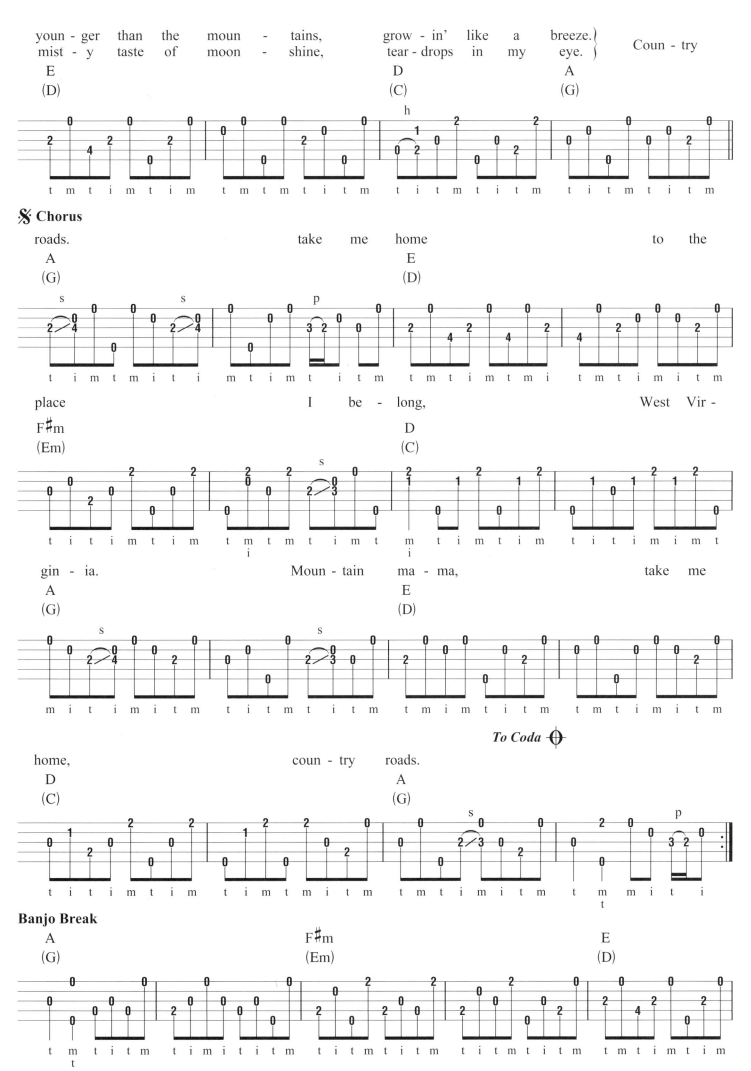

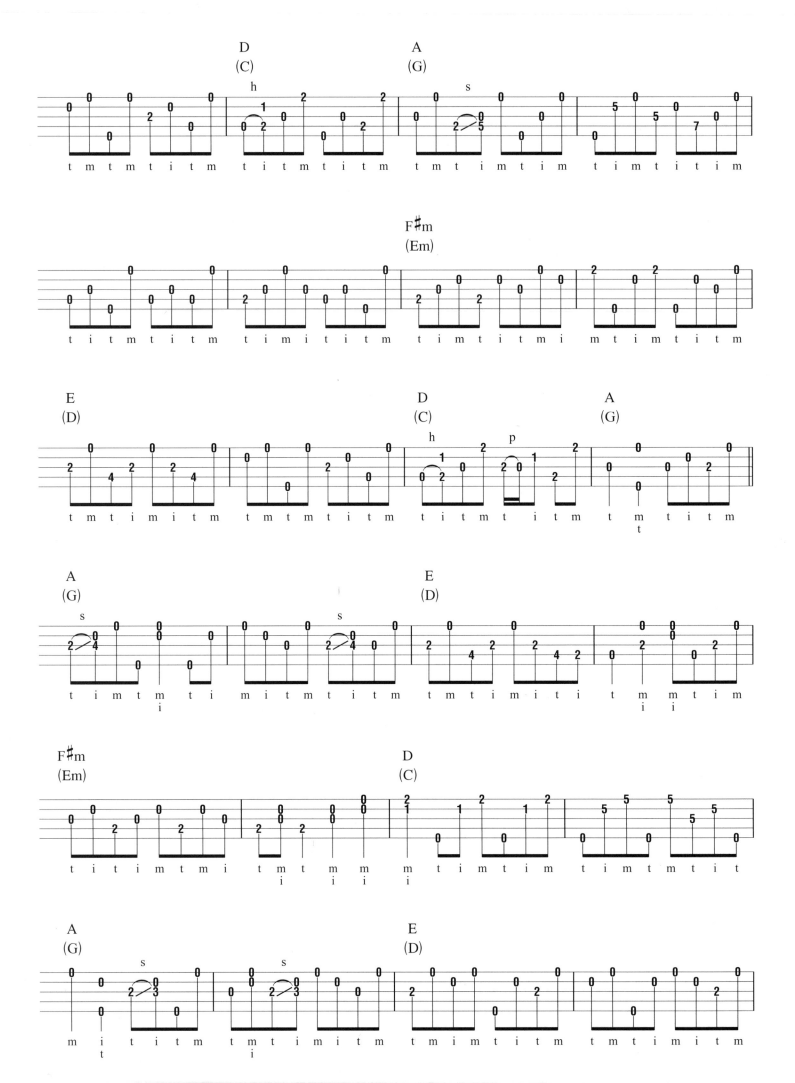

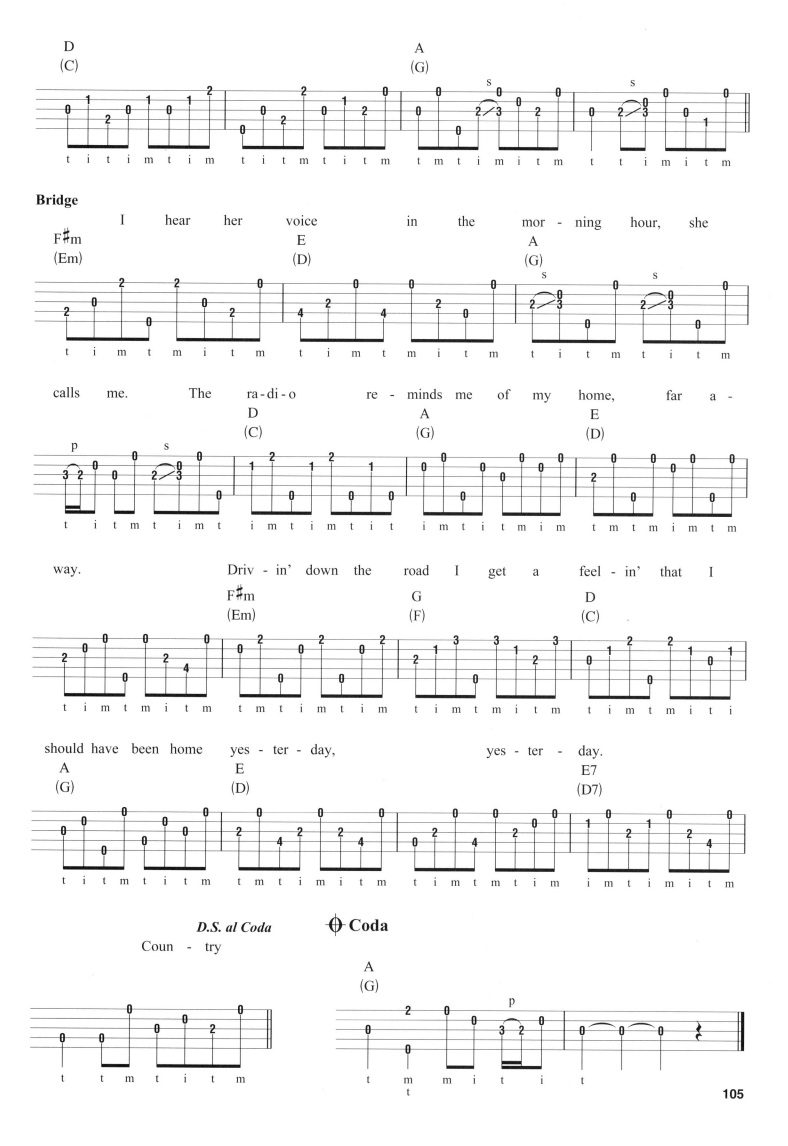

Bridge

I hear her voice in the mor - ning hour, she calls me. The ra - di - o re - minds me of my home, far a - way. Driv - in' down the road I get a feel - in' that I should have been home yes - ter - day, yes - ter - day.

D.S. al Coda   **Coda**

Coun - try

Tennessee Waltz

Words and Music by Redd Stewart and Pee Wee King

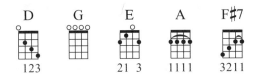

G tuning:
(5th-1st) G-D-G-B-D

Key of D

Verse

Moderately slow

I was danc-ing with my dar-ling to the Ten - ne - see

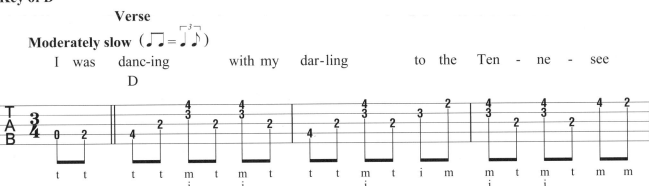

Waltz, when an old friend I hap-pened to see.

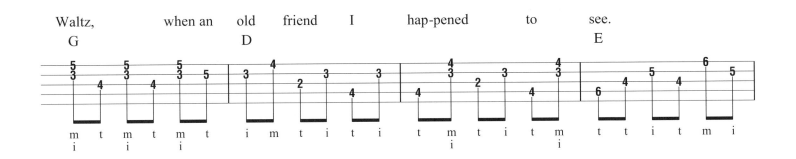

I in-tro-duced him to my loved one and while they were

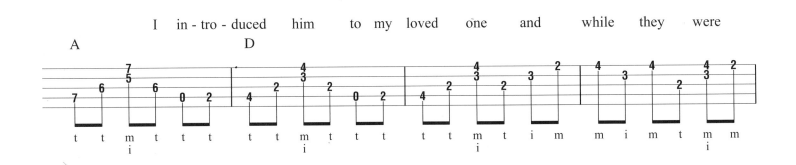

danc-ing, my friend stole my sweet-heart from me. I re-

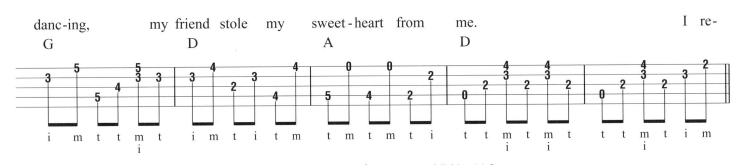

Chorus

mem - ber the night and the Ten - ne - see Waltz, now I

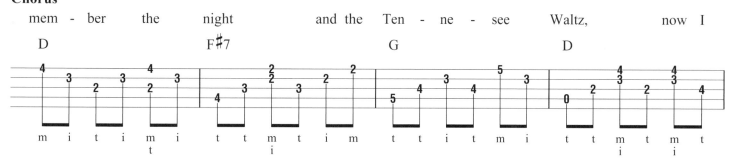

know just how much I have lost. Yes, I

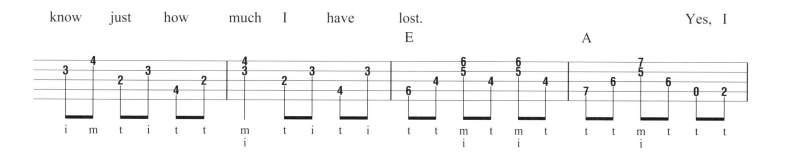

lost my lit - tle dar - lin' the night they were play-ing the

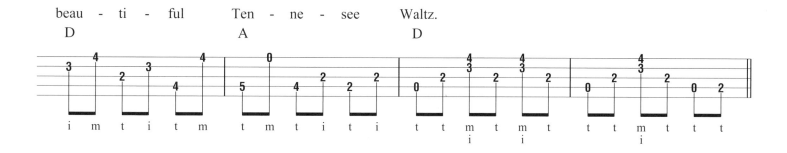

beau - ti - ful Ten - ne - see Waltz.

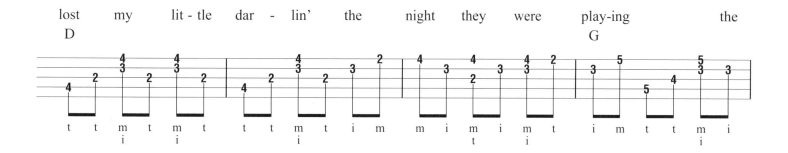

Banjo Break

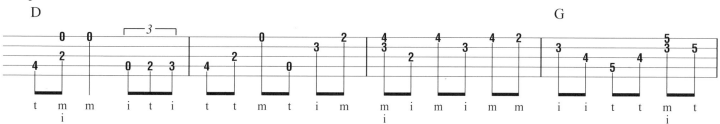

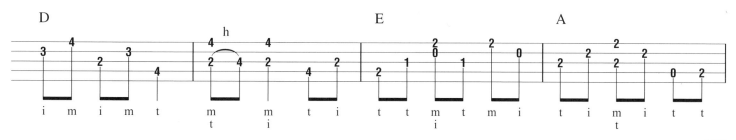

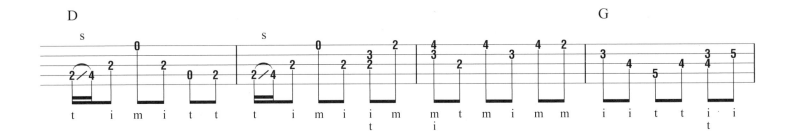

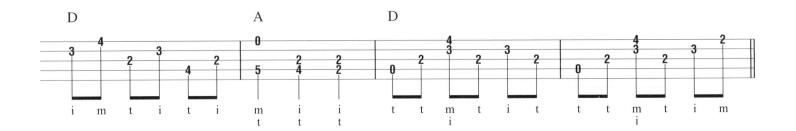

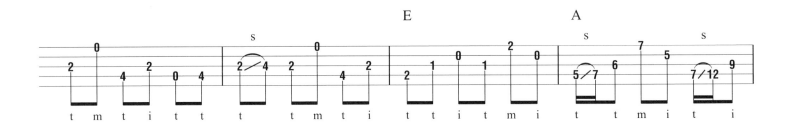

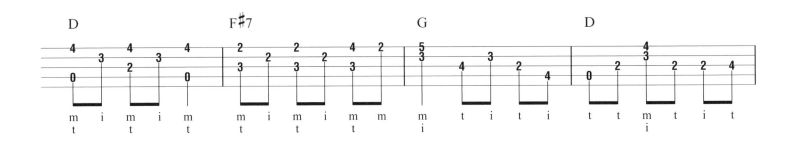

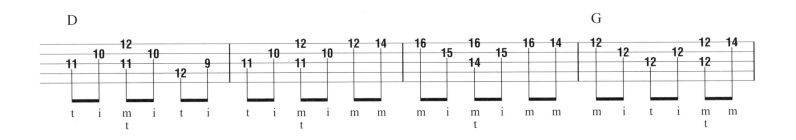

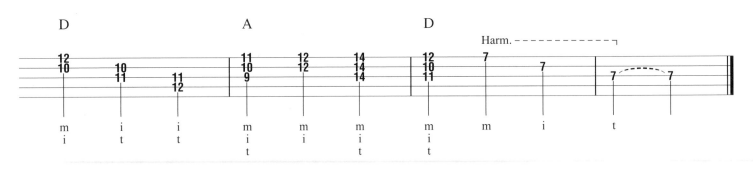

Turkey in the Straw

American Folksong

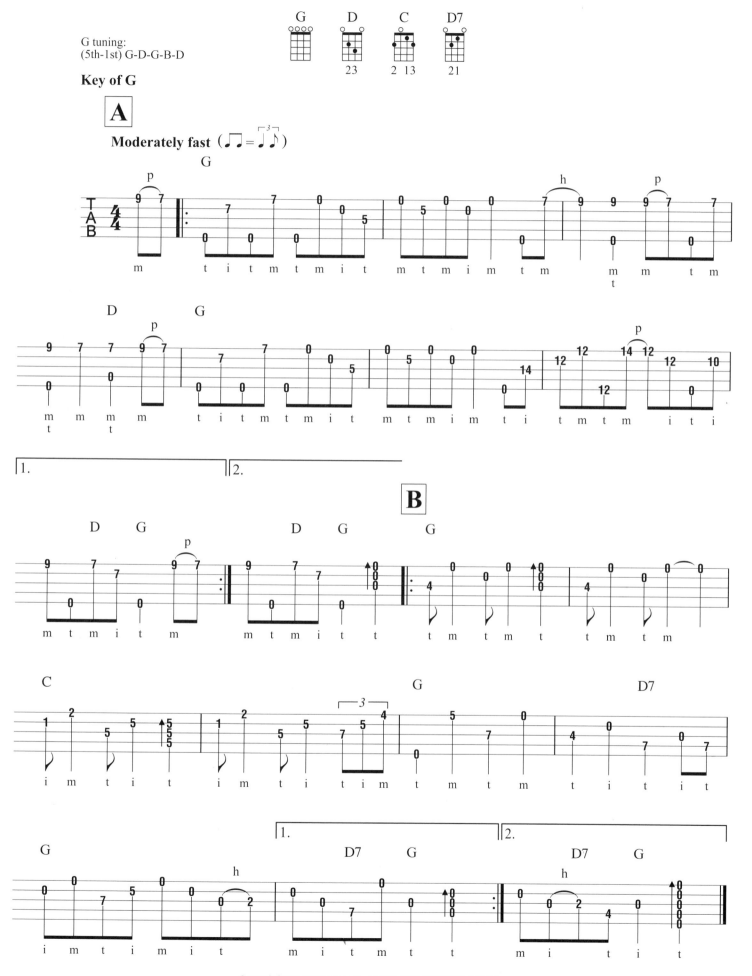

Wildwood Flower

Words and Music by A.P. Carter

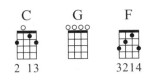

G tuning:
(5th-1st) G-D-G-B-D

Key of C

Verse

Moderately, in 2

Oh, I'll twine with my ming - les and wav - ing black

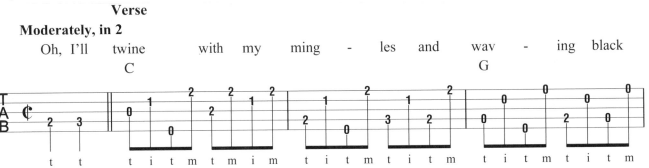

hair with the ros - es so red and the

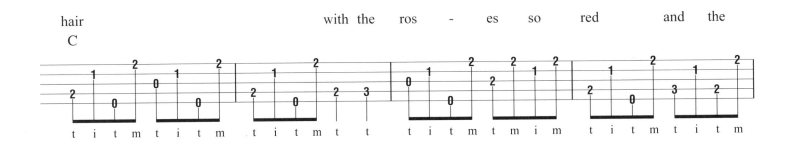

lil - lies so fair, and the myr - tle so

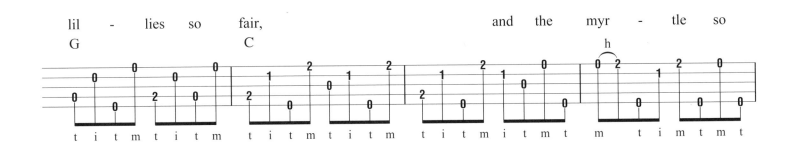

bright with the em - er - ald hue, the pale am - in -

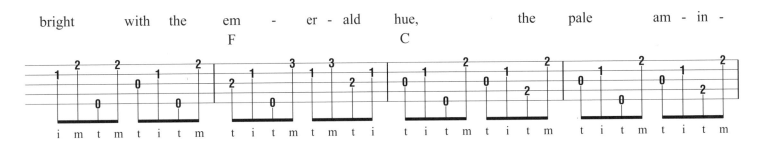

i - ta and vio - lets so blue.

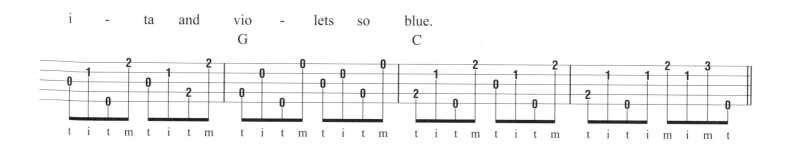

Banjo Break

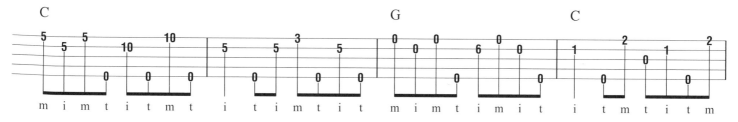

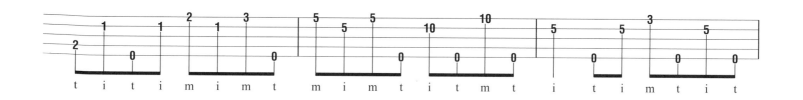

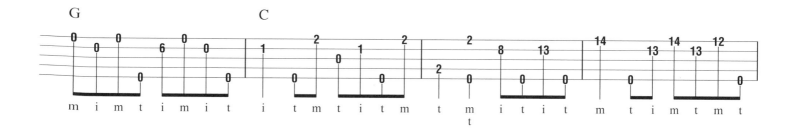

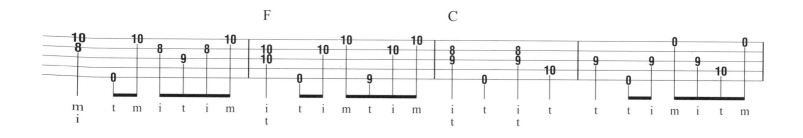

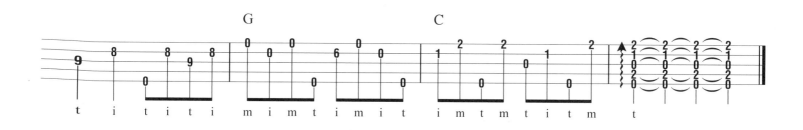

BANJO NOTATION LEGEND

TABLATURE graphically represents the banjo fingerboard. Each horizontal line represents a string, and each number represents a fret.

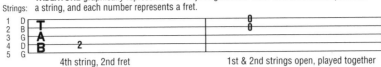

Strings:
1 D
2 B
3 G
4 D
5 G

4th string, 2nd fret   1st & 2nd strings open, played together

TIME SIGNATURE:
The upper number indicates the number of beats per measure, the lower number indicates that a quarter note gets one beat.

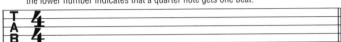

CUT TIME:
Each note's time value should be cut in half. As a result, the music will be played twice as fast as it is written.

QUARTER NOTE:
time value = 1 beat

EIGHTH NOTES:
time value = 1/2 beat each

single   in series

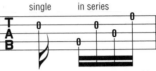

SIXTEENTH NOTES:
time value = 1/4 beat each

single   in series

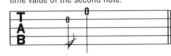

DOTTED QUARTER NOTE:
time value = 1 1/2 beat

TIE: Pick the 1st note only, then let it sustain for the combined time value.

TRIPLET: Three notes played in the same time normally occupied by two notes of the same time value.

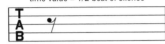

GRACE NOTE: A quickly played note with no time value of its own. The grace note and the note following it only occupy the time value of the second note.

RITARD: A gradual slowing of the tempo or speed of the song.

rit.

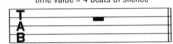

QUARTER REST:
time value = 1 beat of silence

EIGHTH REST:
time value = 1/2 beat of silence

HALF REST:
time value = 2 beats of silence

WHOLE REST:
time value = 4 beats of silence

ENDINGS: When a repeated section has a first and second ending, play the first ending only the first time and play the second ending only the second time.

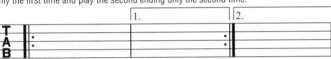

1.   2.

REPEAT SIGNS: Play the music between the repeat signs two times.

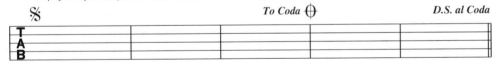

D.S. AL CODA:
Play through the music until you complete the measure labeled *"D.S. al Coda,"* then go back to the sign (𝄋).
Then play until you complete the measure labeled *"To Coda ⊕,"* then skip to the section labeled "⊕ **Coda**."

𝄋   *To Coda* ⊕   *D.S. al Coda*   ⊕ *Coda*

HAMMER-ON: Strike the first (lower) note with one finger, then sound the higher note (on the same string) with another finger by fretting it without picking.

h

PULL-OFF: Place both fingers on the notes to be sounded. Strike the first note and without picking, pull the finger off to sound the second (lower) note.

p

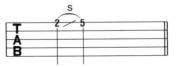

SLIDE UP: Strike the first note and then slide the same fret-hand finger up to the second note. The second note is not struck.

s

SLIDE DOWN: Strike the first note and then slide the same fret-hand finger down to the second note. The second note is not struck.

s

HALF-STEP CHOKE: Strike the note and bend the string up 1/2 step.

1/2

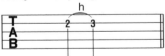

WHOLE-STEP CHOKE: Strike the note and bend the string up one step.

1

NATURAL HARMONIC: Strike the note while the fret-hand lightly touches the string directly over the fret indicated.

Harm.

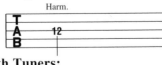

BRUSH: Play the notes of the chord indicated by quickly rolling them from bottom to top.

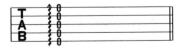

Scruggs/Keith Tuners:

HALF-TWIST UP: Strike the note, twist tuner up 1/2 step, and continue playing.

1/2

HALF-TWIST DOWN: Strike the note, twist tuner down 1/2 step, and continue playing.

1/2

WHOLE-TWIST UP: Strike the note, twist tuner up one step, and continue playing.

1

WHOLE-TWIST DOWN: Strike the note, twist tuner down one step, and continue playing.

1

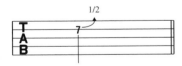

Right Hand Fingerings

t = thumb   i = index finger   m = middle finger